Embracing the Future

A Guide for Reshaping Your Church's Teaching Ministry

Edited by Linda R. Isham

Contributors:

David G. Berube

Deborah J. Blanchard

Linda R. Isham

Beth Keating

Dennis Plourde

Published by Judson Press
for
Witherspoon Press, a ministry of the Presbyterian Church (U.S.A.),
Board of Christian Education of the Cumberland Presbyterian Church,
and
United Church Publishing House of the United Church of Canada

If you are interested in customizing this material for use in training events, you may request a complimentary diskette of the text (minus illustrations and hymns) by writing to:

Victoria McGoey
Judson Press
P. O. Box 851
Valley Forge, PA 19482-0851
Please specify in which format you would like the text files:
WORD or WordPerfect (and which version of WordPerfect).

Library of Congress Cataloging-in-Publication Data

Embracing the future : a guide for reshaping your church's teaching
  ministry / Linda R. Isham, editor ; contributors, David G. Berube
  . . . [et. al.].
     p. cm.
  Includes bibliographical references.
  ISBN 0-8170-1327-X (pbk : alk. paper)
  1. Christian education. 2. Pastoral theology.   I. Isham, Linda
R. II. Berube, David G.
  BV1471.2.E43 1999
  268–dc21   99-11592

Printed in the U.S.A.

06 05 04 03 02 01 00 99

10 9 8 7 6 5 4 3 2 1

Contents

Introduction

This planning guide came about as the result of conversation about the nature and direction of the church's teaching ministry by a small group of New England folks deeply committed to that ministry. They make up the steering committee of the New England Educational Ministries Partnership (NEEMP), a partnership of Educational Ministries, American Baptist Churches, U.S.A., and the five New England Regions (Connecticut, Maine, Massachusetts, Rhode Island, and Vermont/New Hampshire) of the ABC/USA. The group includes region executive ministers, area ministers, local church pastors and ministers of Christian education, other regional staff, laypersons, and one national staff person—a unique mix of people bringing varying perspectives to the table. This group of people helped to shape the vision and the resource itself.

Five people contributed to the writing of the resource. They include David G. Berube, formerly a pastor, and now a freelance writer living on Martha's Vineyard; Deborah J. Blanchard, Director of Marketing for Grotonwood/Oceanwood Camping and Conferencing and Ministry of Christian Education, First Baptist Church, Littleton, Massachusetts; Beth Keating, former area minister for American Baptist Churches of Maine and now director of an after-school program, First Baptist Church, Springvale, Maine, and goat dairy farmer; Dennis Plourde, former pastor in New Hampshire and now serving as a missionary in the Philippines; and Linda R. Isham, Director of Planning for Congregational Education, Educational Ministries, ABC/USA, and Director of Educational Ministries, American Baptist Churches of Connecticut.

Two people from the NEEMP Steering Committee were our chief critics and advocates: Tony Pappas and Judy Pratt. We are grateful for both their pushing and prodding and their support.

We offer this guide as one tool for churches seeking to reclaim or renew a heart for teaching and to reshape their teaching ministries. We have been encouraged by the words of 2 Corinthians 4:1, "Therefore, since it is by God's mercy that we are engaged in this ministry, we do not lose heart." May they be words of encouragement for all who read and use this resource.

Linda R. Isham

CHAPTER 1

Seeing the Big Picture and Getting Started

by Linda R. Isham

PURPOSE:

 take a deeper look at challenges faced in the church's teaching ministry

 overview a planning process to use in getting a church's teaching ministry in shape for a new century

 understand the flexibility of this planning process

 see ways to organize for planning for the future of the teaching ministry

---

Stuart Dent looked around the table at the group assembled to talk about how Old First Church might improve its teaching ministry. Stu, the young adult representative, had been part of these things before. He always came filled with hope but usually walked away disappointed. This time, he determined, cautious optimism was the better course. And as the conversation got started, he believed he had chosen a good approach.

Art Craft came to Old First Church originally to help with summer vacation Bible school. Before the meeting officially began, Art jumped in with what Stu liked to think of as "Craft's motto" because the words were so predictable. "Why should we change such a nice Sunday school program?" Art recited. "It's familiar to the teachers, and every week the children get to make a nice project to take home. Sure the Sunday school is small, but it's only a loss to those who don't come."

"I've been on every committee several times over forty-some years, so I know a thing or two about this church," chimed in Kate Ulater. "We've got bigger things to worry about. Besides, we have trouble recruiting teachers now, and we need new curriculum. And I don't see the congregation agreeing to put more money toward another new curriculum. That's why people elected me to this group—to see that you people make a decision and stick with it."

Oh, that's why, *thought Stu;* Kate—Kat to her friends—agrees to be on committees then only shows up when major decisions are pending. That way she can

defend the way it's always been done and keep us from spending money.

"Mrs. Ulater," Stu found himself responding, "this isn't supposed to be about money. You weren't at our last meeting when we discussed the agenda for tonight. Imogene wants us to look at our teaching ministry—to see how it is now and how we might make it better. I think we should let her start the meeting." Stu heard Pastor Pat grunt and saw a nod. He thought, Not going to jump in yet, are you. Good ole "Stand Pat."

With this tense and tenuous prelude concluded, Imogene Pozibel, newest church member on the committee and its leader, started the first of a series of gatherings to consider Old First Church's teaching ministry. She welcomed the folks, and the journey began.

Christian education in the church today faces many challenges. Often these challenges are described in the following or similar ways: "Attendance in Sunday school is down from last year." "Teachers won't attend teacher meetings and workshops." "We don't have enough teachers to start classes this fall." "Many children attend every other Sunday because their parents are divorced." "We don't seem to be able to attract young adults." "We seem to think that Sunday school is all there is to Christian education and that it's just for kids." We desperately seek solutions, and in our efforts to meet these challenges, we ask for new models, techniques, or curriculum to try. More often than not during times of uncertainty we look for quick fixes, programs, gimmicks, and techniques. Seldom when speaking of the challenges faced in Christian education today do we speak about our need to reclaim a heart for teaching or our need to look deeply at what we are called to do and how we can be most faithful in doing that.

The planning process described in this resource is intended to help churches take a deeper look at the challenges currently being faced and at the same time provide practical steps that can be taken to renew our teaching ministries. This resource can be your "consultant in a book." The planning process takes a faith approach as much as a business and/or educational approach. Each of the seven steps of the plan is accompanied by a refrain of praying, learning, and sharing. This can best be pictured by a diagram that shows the rhythm between the steps and the refrain. See Figure 1 (also available as Reproducible Sheet 1, which can be used for an overhead transparency master or handout).

The deeper look we must take requires open and receptive hearts and minds. It is a prayerful stance that we are asked to take. It calls us to listen to God's voice that we might discern the faithful ways to go, learn from our history and tradition, from today's world, and from those who have found ways that work for this day and have promise for the days ahead. While taking a deeper look may require extra time, it is meant more in the sense of being reflective, thoughtful, and critical (in the good sense of the word). Thus, we start the process when we begin to ask questions about what we currently are doing.

The planning steps and the refrains offered in this resource are meant to help us reclaim a heart for teaching, an idea for which we must give credit to Parker Palmer. He speaks about reclaiming a heart for teaching in his book *The Courage to Teach: Exploring the Inner Landscape of a Teacher's Life.* In chapter 1 he writes: "Good teachers possess a capacity for connectedness.... The connections made by good teachers are held not in their methods but in their hearts— meaning heart in its ancient sense, as the place where intellect and emotion and spirit and will converge in the human self."[1] Just as individual teachers need a heart for teaching, so the church as a community of believers needs a corporate heart for teaching, and where it is lost it can be reclaimed.

Or we might speak about reclaiming our courage to teach. We need to again believe that we have something to teach a world in need of the Good News, in need of community and connectedness, in need of a love that will not let us go. W. Paul Jones speaks of courage in much the same way Palmer uses the word: ". . . *courage* means acting from a faithful, trusting heart. The expression *having the courage of one's convictions* preserves something of this meaning."[2]

Henri Nouwen writes that the heart is the center of our being, and therefore if we have a heart for teaching, we are letting our center speak for and about teaching. Likewise, jazz saxophonist Charlie Parker says, "If it's not in your heart, then it's not in your horn." Of the church we could say, "If it's not in our heart, it's not in our teaching."

One place to learn about such heart and courage to teach is in our history and tradition. Craig Dykstra reminds us of this rich treasury of our past in an article in *Initiatives in Religion,* the newsletter of Lilly Endowment, Inc.: "Individually and in groups, more and more people have taken it on themselves to delve into the Scriptures, to explore the lives and writings of the inspiring saints and thinkers of the church's past (both ancient and recent), and to figure out how to think through current issues with the resources thus brought to bear." As we seek to figure out the ways to do the church's teaching ministry in a new century, we, too, can call upon this *sensus fidelium* (the sense of the faithful). Dykstra goes on to write, ". . . a key test of the church's faithfulness to God—and its significance in the world— will be its capacity to draw upon the riches of its inheritance and the wisdom of all its people in the 'figuring things out' we all have to do. Developing that capacity more strongly is some of the most important work the Christian churches in our society have to do—now."[3]

And it is not just to the past that we are called to look. We are called to be in conversation with one another—within our own congregations and beyond. The learning and sharing components of this planning resource push us to be in touch with others today. Other connections are needed with the church's other ministries and overall planning process. Planning for the church's teaching ministry cannot stand by itself. It needs to be an integral part of the church's overall plan for ministry or renewal. For too long we in the church have tended to look at our Christian education program (often seen only as the Sunday school) by itself, isolated from the rest of the life of the church. Consequently, both the church and its teaching ministry have suffered from such isolation.

Why plan?

We start with four assumptions:
1. Planning is important.
2. It can and should be fun.
3. There is more than one way to go about it.
4. Change is continually taking place, and planning is a faithful and life-giving response to change.

One assumption of this planning resource is that planning for renewal is important and can take time. Thus, a step-by-step process is outlined and described in detail. Many but not all of the steps in this planning process will sound familiar. While those of us who have developed this plan believe it works, it is important to recognize that this plan is just a guide and that its developers assume that those who use it will adapt and personalize it to fit their specific situations. And while it has been tested and used in workshops and in churches, it must be owned and modified by the users for best results.

As for the second assumption, that planning can and should be fun, we have tried to approach the steps in a variety of ways and have included left-brain and right-brain activities—both analytical and creative approaches— plus lots of options. Part of having fun is not taking ourselves too seriously as we plan. We hope that a spirit of

Figure 1

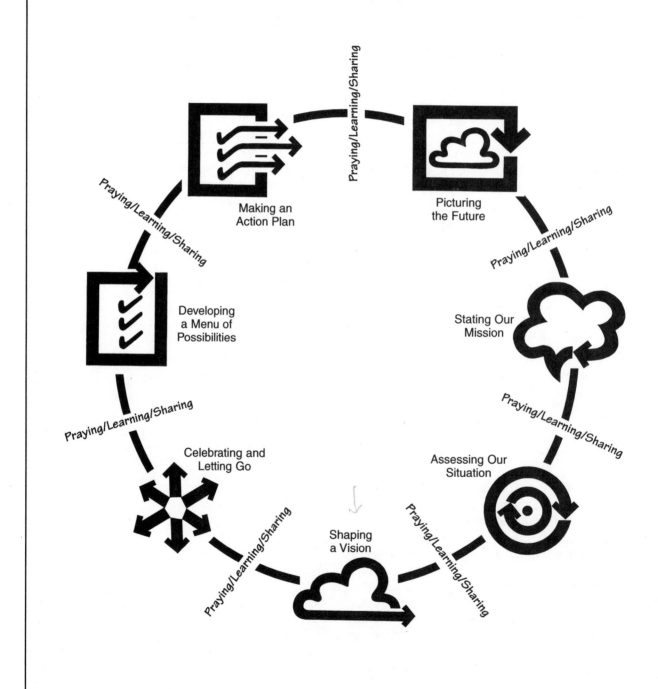

A Guide for Reshaping Your Church's Teaching Ministry

Making an Action Plan

Picturing the Future

Praying/Learning/Sharing

Praying/Learning/Sharing

Praying/Learning/Sharing

Developing a Menu of Possibilities

Stating Our Mission

Praying/Learning/Sharing

Praying/Learning/Sharing

Celebrating and Letting Go

Assessing Our Situation

Praying/Learning/Sharing

Praying/Learning/Sharing

Shaping a Vision

joy, some laughter, and even some jokes will be part of your planning time. And in that spirit we share the cartoon below.

A third assumption is that there is more than one way to go about planning. You may choose to start with any step of this plan, and you may use only some or all of the steps. You may combine some and/or skip others. Each person and/or group has different planning needs, interests, preferences, and skills. We hope that you'll use this resource in ways that enhance the gifts, needs, and interests of your church and planning group. You do not exist for this planning process; it exists for you.

Finally, this planning process is based on the assumption that change has been and is continually going on. This is true in the church and in Christian education as in all of life. Even if we do nothing, change is taking place, so why not work in bringing about renewal that is faithful to our calling? The plan also recognizes that there are circumstances, traditions, and experiences that make change, whether planned or not, difficult and sometimes painful.

Marjorie J. Thompson, in her book *Soul Feast,* offers helpful insight about change and Christian tradition: "Many in the church today view Christian tradition as impeding creative change. But the irony is that the truest aspects of Christian tradition are the most radically creative and life-changing. Indeed, tradition itself provides us with criteria for 'sorting living truths from dying customs.'"[4] As we seek to make changes, it is important to distinguish between living truths and dying customs. The appreciative inquiry approach focuses on what is working and valuing the best of "what is" in order to envision "what might be."

What are the planning steps we can take?

We have pictured the seven steps in this planning process in a circle (see Fig. 1), suggesting movement and the possibility of beginning a planning process with any of the seven steps. One logical order to use is the following (and incidently the order of the remaining chapters, each focusing on a planning step): Picturing the Future, Stating Our Mission, Assessing Our Situation, Shaping a Vision, Celebrating and Letting Go, Developing a Menu of Possibilities, and Making an Action Plan. But you may start at any one of the seven steps and even omit any that don't fit your needs. For example, if you have just spent time reviewing your church's Christian education mission statement, you may want to begin with Assessing Our Situation. Or perhaps you work best by beginning with strategies. In that case, start with Developing a Menu of Possibilities.

As was stated earlier, the developers of this planning process view it as a "consultant in a book" to be used as a tool by a given faith community as it seeks to renew its teaching ministry (note that we use "teaching ministry" and "Christian education" interchangeably). "Rather than depending on specialists, the community—which, after all, will have to live with any new development—is involved as much as possible in the planning."[5] This statement was made about how a city works with architects on development projects, but its meaning is applicable to a church planning its future teaching ministry. It is important to involve in the planning the people who will implement the program.

Pontius' Puddle

WORKING ALONE, IT TOOK GOD ONLY 7 DAYS TO FORM THE WORLD. BUT COOPERATING WITH THOSE WHO BELIEVE, GOD REQUIRED 700,000 DAYS TO BUILD THE CHURCH.

THEREFORE WE CAN ASSUME THAT THE CHURCH IS GOD'S MOST GLORIOUS CREATION!

EITHER THAT, OR DON'T DO THINGS BY COMMITTEE.

Congregations may reprint this strip by noting its source and sending $10 to Joel Kauffmann, 111 Carter Road, Goshen, IN 46526.

Let's now look briefly at each of the steps in the order given in this resource. You will note an icon in front of each step. That same icon will appear at the start of the chapter related to that step.

Picturing the Future

From the beginning, this process is intended to be future-directed, so it is important that we set our minds and hearts in that direction. This can be seen as a stage-setting step for all the others. Before looking at our current situation, we must push ourselves to dream, to picture what we would like to see in the future for our church's teaching ministry. When it is exciting and working well, what will it look like, what will be happening, what will be the results, and what will it take to get there? This is a step for gathering quick impressions, for using as much as possible the right brain and one's creativity. While it can set the stage for later work done in shaping a vision, it doesn't take the work that far. Its intent is to get us thinking and feeling future, to look ahead, to move out of the present, to get some glimpses of some future realities or possibilities.

This is both an individual and a communal activity. While we are called to do our own picturing, we are also called to share these pictures with one another and build a communal picture of the future of our church's teaching ministry.

Stating Our Mission

A mission statement describes our purpose or reason for being. When the developers of this resource were first working together to build a common understanding, we said that a mission statement should tell why we exist. It should be foundational and speak more in generalities than in specifics and should stand the test of time. Some experts in the field suggest that a mission statement should last one hundred years![6]

Mission statements help us clearly and quickly express what we are about. They serve as a good starting point for developing goals and objectives, help us evaluate programs and ministries, and help us determine priorities. In short, they can help us keep on track.

Assessing Our Situation

At this point (or at some point) in the planning process, it is important to take a careful look at what we currently are doing in our teaching ministry, what is working well, what could be working better, where the gaps are, what our greatest challenges are, and what resources we have. We can and need to do this assessing at several levels and with as many people as possible, both those involved and those who are marginally involved or not involved at all. This chapter deals with assessing our church, our teaching ministry, and the world. It includes practical helps and tools.

This assessment takes us beyond the walls of the church into the community in which we are called to teach to gather information on the demographics and needs of the community. Sources of help for such community assessment are suggested.

Shaping a Vision

For our purposes vision differs from mission in the following ways. It is future-oriented, speaking from the reason we exist in terms of what we do now and in the future. It is more particular for a given time and speaks more about how we'll do that to which we are called.

Shaping a vision can help us build a bridge from the challenging and sometimes bewildering present into the future. A vision for the future gives legs to a mission statement. It grows from a rich past, having roots in what has gone before. Yet it points us to the future and keeps us from focusing on or being bound to the past. A vision is hopeful and filled with promise.

The chapter on shaping a vision offers some examples and suggests a process to use in shaping a vision.

Celebrating and Letting Go

This planning process values a congregation's past and at the same time recognizes that sometimes it is hard to let go of parts of that past. This step in the plan is intended to help a church pause and celebrate its teaching ministry, the good and the not so good. Communal celebrations are suggested, because recognition cannot happen individually. As we remember and give thanks for all that has happened in our teaching ministry over the years, we give opportunity to let go of those things that we need to let go of if we are to move courageously into the future. There is a sense in which we are called to come together as a community and share our disappointments and fears. Once we have acknowledged them, we can let go of them, turning them over to God.

Often in our planning we dismiss the need to look to our past and the varying and conflicting feelings we have regarding it. Failing to celebrate the past or to acknowledge those things of the past to which we cling can block our moving ahead into the future to which God is calling us. This step is intended to help us deal with those parts of the past that hinder and those that enhance our planning for the future of the church's teaching ministry.

Developing a Menu of Possibilities

In this step we begin to list all the possible directions we might take—thus building a menu of possible teaching ministry actions, ministries, and programs. The work on mission and vision statements and assessment of our situation should all feed helpfully into this step. This step should produce a list of possible actions, programs, and/or ministries that can help us carry out our mission in the way our vision for the future suggests.

Making an Action Plan

An action plan states the specific steps we will take to carry out our priority actions, programs, and/or ministries, tells who is responsible for each step, and sets a time schedule for each step. Evaluation is built into the action plan. The chapter dealing with making an action plan begins with help for prioritizing your list of possible actions, programs, and/or ministries. It addresses the value of experimentation in some situations and also offers some examples and tips for making this step in the plan work. As we make an action plan, we should keep in mind that as a people of faith we don't need all the pieces carefully in place in order to act. We need to leave room for mystery and flexibility.

We are reminded that planning is only the beginning. Planning without implementation of the plan is a fruitless activity. Planning leads to implementation which leads to planning and thus we have a cycle that is repeated or continuous.

What about implementation?

This resource describes a planning process. The developers believe that it is evocative, helpful, and constructive. But it is only a planning process. It needs to be followed by an *implementation* process. First you plan. Then you do. Do not stop your efforts when you have completed the planning cycle. Implement!

An implementation cycle has the following steps:

1. *Work the action plan.* Do what you planned to do. Release people to do what energized them in the planning phase. Procure the needed resources. Change what you need to change to move from your past into God's future.

2. *Monitor and evaluate.* As you put your nose to the grindstone of implementation, remember to keep one moistened finger up in the wind. Ask, "How is it going? What is working? What didn't fly? What and how do we need to change the original action plan? What would we change the next time around?"

3. *Adapt.* Modify your action plan and/or strategies and procedures within it based on what you have learned in steps 1 and 2 above.

Cycle through steps 1, 2, and 3 of your implementation during the life cycle of your annual educational program, and then again and again. It takes time to establish new approaches in the life and rhythm of a congregation. Think in terms of a three-to-five-year time frame to establish a new approach. Remember that year after year of "tweaking" an action plan will render you off the original target eventually. Remember, too, that new people will be added to your group and others will be leaving. Giving attention to changes in leadership and ways to bring new people on board is important. We suggest that you go back through a planning cycle in the fourth or fifth year, using evaluations from the previous implementation cycle. The frequency of recycling may well depend on the length of terms of office and your church's overall planning cycle.[7]

The relationship between the implementation and planning cycles is described in Figure 2.

Figure 2

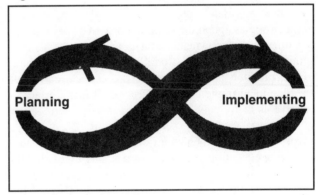

Planning   Implementing

Why the "Praying, Learning, Sharing" refrain?

This threefold refrain of praying, learning, and sharing appears between each step of the plan to undergird each step and to provide breathing space. It reminds us that praying, learning (from the Bible, the world, and others), and sharing (by both involving and communicating) with the larger congregation of which we are a part are integral to the planning and not just something we do at the beginning and end like giving an invocation and benediction. The idea is for a planning group to establish a rhythm between the planning steps and the refrain. Each chapter contains specific ideas for praying, learning, and sharing related to the particular step described in that chapter.

The refrain resources that appear following this first chapter are intended to guide you as you prepare to enter into this planning process and as you conclude it and enter the implementation cycle. Using the threefold refrain now as you prepare for this planning process will give you experience in using prayer, learning, and sharing with the congregation and help you see the best way to integrate them in your own planning.

What if we need more help or want to offer our comments?

Each chapter includes a resources page following the refrain pages. We have sought to list resources that are readily available.

You will also find at the end of each chapter a page asking for your comments on this resource. We are eager for you to tell us how you used this resource, what was helpful and not helpful, and what you were able to accomplish.

How can we use this resource?

This planning process can guide you in planning your total teaching ministry or one part of that ministry, such as children's ministry, vacation Bible school, or a small-group Bible study ministry. In fact, it can be used to plan most any church ministry.

An appropriate group to guide the planning process is the group assigned the responsibility of your church's teaching ministry, whether that is a committee, board, ministry group, or task force. Such a body can initiate, guide, monitor, and evaluate the process and carry out the plan in an implementation process. It is important to involve as many people and groups in the congregation as possible, especially people who are likely to be involved in implementation. It is important for this Christian education planning group to stay in touch with the church's governing board so that the teaching ministry is seen and included as a significant ministry in the total life of the church and so that it does not go off on its own at cross purposes to the church. The church is incomplete without the teaching ministry, and the teaching ministry is incomplete without the church.

Getting organized

1. Spend time in prayer and study to discern God's call to renew your church's teaching ministry.

2. Determine where in the process you will begin, in what order you will take each step, how many steps you will use, and how you will incorporate the refrain components.

3. Choose someone to lead the planning process and assign specific steps. Make assignments on the basis of the number of people you have involved and their gifts, interests, or passions.

4. Develop an initial time line with built-in check points. Monitor your progress so you know when to modify the process and your timetable. Don't let it drag out too long or people will lose interest. Consider doing some steps simultaneously.

5. Report to your church's governing board on progress to date.

6. Communicate with the congregation about the planning you are beginning and invite their participation.

7. Order, duplicate, and prepare necessary resources.

8. Have fun!

Notes

1. Parker J. Palmer, *The Courage to Teach: Exploring the Inner Landscape of a Teacher's Life* (San Francisco: Jossey-Bass Publishers, 1998), 11.

2. W. Paul Jones, "Courage as the Heart of Faith," *Weavings* (May–June 1997), 9.

3. Craig Dykstra, "Figuring Things Out," *Initiatives in Religion* (Lilly Endowment, Inc., Winter 1998), 2.

4. Marjorie J. Thompson, *Soul Feast* (Louisville: Westminster John Knox, 1995), 13.

5. Francesca Lyman, "Twelve Gates to the City," *Sierra* (May–June 1997), 30–31.

6. James C. Collins and Jerry I. Porras, "Building Your Company's Vision," *Harvard Business Review* (September–October 1996), 68.

7. This understanding of implementation comes from Anthony G. Pappas, Old Colony Area Minister, American Baptist Churches of Massachusetts.

Praying...
for Seeing the Big Picture and Getting Started

Enter into prayer
    with grateful hearts
    as listeners
        seeking to discern God's will for your
        church's teaching ministry.

Remember the words of Dom John Chapman:
        "The only way to pray is to pray; and the
        way to pray well is to pray much."

Invite others in your congregation to be in prayer with you, to join you as prayer partners.

Use any or all of the following prayer resources or those from your own rich storehouse.

- Offer your gifts—your skills, passions, and expertise—to God.
  (As you prepare to plan and then later as you prepare to implement your action plan.)
  — Individually identify skills, passions, and areas of expertise
  — Share these out loud
  — Share together in the Lord's Supper and sing "Let Us Talents and Tongues Employ"

- Read this poem as your prayer.

  Listening, Learning

  Often I look around
  and compare myself
  to others;
  I see myself lacking,
  ordinary.

  But I turn to Scripture,
  I hear good news!
  In God's creative plan,
  grace is varied,
  and each is gifted
  for service.

  As I lean toward God
  and listen
  in prayer's process.
  I am aware
  that ordinary
  can be transformed
  as it is given to God
  and given away.
  Praise God
  for varied grace!

  Roberta Porter (*Alive Now*, March/April 1997, 33).
  Used by permission.

- Bread is the sustenance of life. When we speak of bread, we mean both physical and spiritual bread.
  — Invite persons present to focus on one phrase from the Lord's Prayer: "Give us this day our daily bread. . . ."
  — Ask, "What bread do you/we need in order to be faithfully and fully involved in the planning process that lies ahead?" And then as you prepare to implement your action plan, ask, "What bread do you/we need in order to be faithfully and fully involved in the implementation process that lies ahead?"
  — Invite participants to share that bread one at a time until everyone who wants to share has had the opportunity to share.
  — Then recite together the Lord's Prayer.

- Sing the spiritual "Standing in the Need of Prayer."

  When finished singing, spend some time in silence, individually listening for direction and guidance from God. As people are ready, invite individuals to speak their prayers out loud.

Let Us Talents and Tongues Employ

Fred Kaan, 1975

Jamaican Folk Melody
Adapt. Doreen Potter, 1975

1. Let us tal - ents and tongues em - ploy, Reach - ing out with a shout of joy:
2. Christ is a - ble to make us one, At the ta - ble He sets the tone,
3. Je - sus calls us in, sends us out Bear - ing fruit in a world of doubt,

Bread is bro - ken, the wine is poured, Christ is spo - ken and seen and heard.
Teach - ing peo - ple to live to bless, Love in word and in deed ex - press.
Gives us love to tell, bread to share: God (Im - man - u - el) ev - ery - where!

Je - sus lives a - gain, earth can breathe a - gain, pass the Word a - round: loaves a - bound!

Words: Fred Kaan
Music: Doreen Potter

Embracing the Future: A Guide for Reshaping Your Church's Teaching Ministry

Standing in the Need of Prayer

Arr. Olive J. Williams

Learning...
for Seeing the Big Picture and Getting Started

LEARNING

Enter into learning
    with open minds and hearts
    as teachers
       and
    students.

Remember the words of Nelson Mandela, "Education is the most powerful weapon you can use to change the world."

Invite others to join you.
Use any of the following resources or techniques or those from your own rich storehouse.

From the Bible:

Read any or all of the following passages: Deuteronomy 6:1-9; Matthew 28:19-20; Ephesians 4:11-13 and reflect on them in terms of your hopes for the future of your church's teaching ministry.

From Christian tradition:

Too often our memories are limited to our experience, our lifetime. They too often don't reach back far enough. Elie Wiesel says it well: "We have to remember that we can't remember. My fear really is that memory itself is in exile. The only possible salvation of the Jewish people is to remember our whole experience. But this memory is so powerful, so exalted, that we can't remember fully: It is bigger than us, bigger than all of us, than all the people . . . memory must go back until it goes back to the source of memory" (from "We Are All Witnesses: An Interview with Elie Wiesel," in *Parabola*, "Myth and the Quest for Meaning," vol. 10, no. 2 [1985]).

- Look back at your church's history, in particular at how teaching has taken place since the founding of your church. Read a history of your church or search through your church's historical records. Develop a Christian education time line for your church.

- Research the history of Christian education in your denomination. Contact your denomination's regional or national office. See the listing of national denominational offices at the back of this resource.

- Study *teaching* in the biblical record. One way to approach this is to use a Bible concordance and look up all the references to the following: *taught,*

teach, teacher, teachers, teaches, teaching, and *teachings.*

- Review the history of the Sunday church school. See this chapter's resource list for a resource to help you.

From today's world:
Choose one of the following books to read and discuss. See this chapter's **RESOURCES** for detailed information on these titles:

- *Dancing with Dinosaurs: Ministry in a Hostile and Hurting World*

- *How to Reach Secular People*

From others:

- Check your denomination's web page for ideas or sources of information on creative planning for the future.

- Check the web pages of other churches for ideas or sources of information on future planning.

- Call your judicatory office and ask for the names of churches doing innovative programming in the area of Christian education or involved in planning for the future.

- Call other churches in your community to see what challenges they are facing and to see if they have found new and/or innovative ways to meet those challenges. Also check to see who else is involved in planning for the future or is interested in such planning.

- Once you have some names of churches, choose ones with whom you wish to talk. Call and arrange a phone conversation or meeting with a few people at each of those now on your list. Ask them questions such as:
  What prompted you to begin this planning process?
  — Describe your process.
  — What resources have helped you?
  — Who is involved and who guides the process?
  — What hints would you give a church just beginning such a process?

- Reflect on these conversations and note implications for your situation.

Sharing...
for Seeing the Big Picture and Getting Started

Be prepared to share with the larger congregation
your plans for envisioning teaching in a new
century and to tell them
the ways you hope to involve them,
how you will keep them posted on progress.

Remember the words of Francesca Lyman, ". . . the
community—which, after all, will have to live with any
new development—is involved as much as possible
in the planning."

Use any or all of the following ways to communicate
with the congregation as you get started (and as you
enter into the implementation phase later) or draw on
your own rich storehouse of ideas:

- Include regular paragraphs in your church
  newsletter and weekly worship bulletin.

- If your church has a web site, include information
  there. Update it regularly.

- Arrange an area on a church bulletin board
  where up-to-date information will be posted.

- Ask your pastor to preach a series of sermons
  related to the church's teaching ministry and the
  importance of looking to the future.

- Present a "moment for ministry" in a service of
  worship, when you briefly tell about your work
  and invite the congregation to join you in this
  work.

- Visit older children's, youth, and adult classes or
  groups and tell them what you are planning and
  how you hope they'll be involved.

- Make it a point to make a presentation at each
  of the church's key boards or committees, including the session or church council.

- List the members of the planning team in as
  many places as possible.

- Invite church members to become prayer partners with the planning team.

- Set up an information table at key church events.

- Tell your friends and family.

Resources...
for Seeing the Big Picture and Getting Started

General Resources

Foster, Charles R., *Educating Congregations: The Future of Christian Education,* (Nashville: Abingdon Press, 1994). A look at what's wrong with some helpful suggestions for correcting the problems. Addresses making meaning, building community, and nurturing hope.

Harris, Maria and Gabriel Moran, *Reshaping Religious Education: Conversations on Contemporary Practice,* (Louisville: Westminster John Knox, 1998). Written conversationally, this book addresses such foundational issues as curriculum, aims, and teaching plus development and spirituality.

Isham, Linda R., *Charting Our Course: Renewing the Church's Teaching Ministry,* (Valley Forge, Pa.: Judson Press, 1997). A view to some things the church can be doing as it seeks to renew its teaching ministry. Filled with practical helps.

Moran, Gabriel, *Showing How: The Act of Teaching,* (Harrisburg, Pa.: Trinity Press International, 1997). Insights into the meaning of "to teach."

Morris, Danny E. and Charles M. Olsen, *Discerning God's Will Together: A Spiritual Practice for the Church,* (Nashville: Upper Room Books, 1997). Presents a discernment model usable in small groups and congregations.

Palmer, Parker J., *The Courage to Teach: Exploring the Inner Landscape of a Teacher's Life,* (San Francisco: Jossey-Bass, 1998). Opens a door to finding the courage and heart to teach in a day that focuses so much on techniques.

Pazmiño, Robert W., *By What Authority Do We Teach? Sources for Empowering Christian Educators,* (Grand Rapids: Baker, 1994). The author defines what authority is and how it is perceived. He applies these factors and the need for confident, authoritative teachers to the ministry of Christian education.

Seymour, Jack L., editor, *Mapping Christian Education: Approaches to Congregational Learning,* (Nashville: Abingdon Press, 1997). Exploration of four themes: transformation, faith community, spiritual growth, and religious instruction.

Prayer Resources

Alive Now, bimonthly devotional magazine published by The Upper Room, Nashville. To order call 1-800-925-6847.

The Secret Place, devotions for daily worship, published quarterly by American Baptist Churches and Christian Board (Disciples of Christ). To order call 1-800-458-3766 (American Baptists) or 1-800-366-3383 (Disciples of Christ).

Thompson, Marjorie J., *Soul Feast,* Louisville: Westminster John Knox, 1995. A helpful look at several Christian spiritual disciplines including prayer.

Weavings, bimonthly journal of the Christian spiritual life published by The Upper Room, Nashville. To order call 1-800-925-6847.

Learning Resources

Easum, William, *Dancing with Dinosaurs: Ministry in a Hostile and Hurting World,* (Nashville: Abingdon Press, 1993). Challenges many of our assumptions about why, when, where, and how we do ministry within the church and mission beyond.

From Sunday School to Church School: Continuities in Protestant Church Education in the U.S. 1860–1929 (Washington, D.C.: University Press of America, 1982). A resource to help you explore the history of the Sunday school movement.

Hunter, George G., *How to Reach Secular People,* (Nashville: Abingdon Press, 1992). A guide to understanding and engaging secular people.

Kohlenberger, John R. III, editor, *The Concise Concordance to the New Revised Standard Version,* (New York: Oxford University Press, 1993). This concordance or another like it can help you locate Scripture references *to taught, teach, teacher, teaching.*

Comment Sheet

We are eager to learn from users what has been helpful, has worked or not, or could have worked better, as well as what you have been able to accomplish with the help of this resource. Please take a few minutes to respond to the following questions and then send them to the address listed below. Use additional pages as needed.

1. These comments are in response to the following steps/chapters
   [please check the appropriate step(s) or chapter(s)]:
   ___ Seeing the Big Picture and Getting Started
   ___ Picturing the Future
   ___ Stating Our Mission
   ___ Assessing Our Situation
   ___ Shaping a Vision
   ___ Celebrating and Letting Go
   ___ Developing a Menu of Possibilities
   ___ Making an Action Plan

2. The most helpful part of this step in the planning process was . . .

3. The least helpful part of this step in the planning process was . . .

4. Changes you should consider are . . .

5. Consider adding the following resource(s) to the resource list:

6. Our key accomplishments related to this step of the planning process are . . .

7. Additional comments:

Thanks! Please return your comments to: Marcia Jessen, Educational Ministries, ABC/USA, P.O. Box 851, Valley Forge, PA 19482-0851; 610-768-2056 FAX; marcia.jessen@abc-usa.org

CHAPTER 2

Picturing the Future

by Deborah J. Blanchard

(handwritten note: deb p23)

PURPOSE:

✔ give permission and freedom to dream and discover new possibilities for a church's teaching ministry

✔ capture some initial pictures of what that future teaching ministry might look like

---

"First of all," Imogene Pozibel framed the opening dialog, "I'd like for us to talk for a while about what we all think of our current teaching ministry. What do we like about what we're doing, and what could be better? And, most importantly, what would we like to see our ministry look like in ten or twenty years? What are our dreams for this ministry? Remember, when we dream there are no boundaries, so dream big!"

(handwritten note: 10 min)

Picturing the future can be fun. It is a time for visioning, dreaming, using our imaginations. There are no boundaries, no limits, no parameters. And there will be no evaluation of our visioning. We are at a new frontier and hold in our thoughts infinite possibilities of new ministries. The Holy Spirit shall be poured out and we shall prophesy, see visions, and dream dreams. The only thing we will not hear nor need say is "We've never done it this way before."

So relax, take a deep breath, ask God to be present, and know that you will be filled with the Holy Spirit to guide you. In a minute we're going to head toward picturing the future of the church's teaching ministry, but first let's spend some time with Moses.

Gilead as far as Dan

Imagine that we're standing on the mountaintop with Moses as he is looking off into the future. It is at the end of his forty-year journey and just before Israel makes it into the Promised Land. It is a liminal[1] moment, an in-between time. Moses is standing on the threshold of something new but has not yet crossed over and stepped through.

Use your imagination and picture Moses standing on the top of Mount Nebo, looking out as far as his eyes can see. He sees pretty far ahead.

> The LORD showed him the whole land: Gilead as far as Dan, all Naphtali, the land of Ephraim and Manasseh, all the land of Judah as far as the Western Sea, the Negeb, and the Plain—that is, the valley of Jericho, the city of palm trees—as far as Zoar. The LORD said to him, 'This is the land of which I swore to Abraham, to Isaac, and to Jacob, saying, "I will give it to your descendants"; I have let you see it with your eyes, but you shall not cross over there.' (Deuteronomy 34:1-4, NRSV)

It took a long time for Moses to get to the edge of the Promised Land. He had worked hard along the way. There were successes and setbacks, triumphs and tragedies, with a good group of people who liked to grumble every now and then. One day they believed and proclaimed their faith, the next day they were complaining again. But Moses never gave up on them and never lost sight of the vision promised by God. He had traveled with them this far, taught them, and cared for them. And now he had to turn the leadership over to someone else. It was time for a new thing.

I wonder what Moses "saw" while standing there on the mountaintop. What was God showing him? What vision was forming before his eyes? What pictures were drawn in his mind? Do you think he wanted to turn around and go back? Were his thoughts hopeful thoughts? Was he imagining what the community of Israel would look like in a few years? In twenty? In fifty? Would they meet new people in this new land? What would Israel be doing? Would they build houses and finally stop living in tents? What would the community do together to survive? Build, plant, teach, harvest, share, and learn? Would they remember why they were God's community? Would they remain faithful and faith-filled?

On the Mountaintop

Materials Needed: Bible
Time Needed: 15–20 minutes

Read Deuteronomy 34:1-4.

Invite those present to close their eyes and imagine they are on the mountaintop with Moses during this liminal moment.

Instruct them to look ahead.

Ask: What do you see? Who do you see? Why?

Have them keep their eyes closed a little longer. Suggest they let their minds wander.

With a new century upon us, the teaching ministry of the church is also standing on the verge of something new. It is a liminal time for the church. We embrace the past and look toward the future. Liminality has been described as a time when "one moves from what was, to the fullness of what is yet to be."[2] And so, like Moses, we too must look toward the future and make new plans.

This chapter includes exercises or activities that can be used with planning groups or other designated groups in a church to help you picture the future. These activities are found in shaded boxes (such as "On the Mountaintop") throughout these pages. Pick and choose those that are appropriate for your situation.

Your church, town, as far as the world

Take a few moments to imagine with me.

You are standing on a mountaintop. You can see very far ahead. You can see that the terrain looks like it could be tough. You are wondering about the future teaching ministry of the church. Imagine all kinds of new ways that children can learn. Imagine the children. Are they faithful and faith-filled? What do they look like? What are they doing?

Imagine a group of children gathering from a number of churches in your community for a field trip on a Tuesday afternoon. They are going to go to an aquarium where they will see exquisite fish with brilliant colors and imaginative shapes. On the way, they learn how God created the fish of the sea, or about Jonah, or about the disciples filling their nets with fish. They sing together, they share a meal together, they talk about how amazing and creative God was and is. They talk about how to care for God's earth. They make new friends. They experience

an "ah-ha" moment and are assured of God's presence and love for them and are faith-filled.

Now imagine youth. Who are they? What is going on in their lives and their hearts? Imagine that once a week they log onto your church's website and complete an interactive lesson—this week it's on the feeding of the five thousand. They read the story, link to a site where they see the hillside where Jesus took the fish and the bread and provided enough for all. At a designated time, the young people log into a private chat room filled with youth from different parts of the country and the world. Youth from Pittsburgh, Podolsk, Dublin, Kinshasa, Beijing, and Lima chat together about the feeding of the five thousand. The church youth leader who is steadfastly involved with these youth joins in. They all have very different perspectives and have a lively discussion! They wrestle with all the issues of the story and discuss issues of world hunger. Two of the young people have experienced hunger in their lives. There is much to share. They decide to do something in their own communities about world hunger. Later in the week all the local youth meet Friday night for pizza and discussion. They decide to help with the food pantry and find out more about hunger issues in their state.

In such a moment of serving, young persons see the love of Christ in the eyes of those being helped and are assured of God's presence and love for them. This experience begins to change how they live their lives, how they interact with others, and how they see the world.

Now imagine adults. Who are they? What is going on in their lives and hearts? Imagine that they have a great hunger for learning. They gather together at 6:00 on Monday mornings before work for Bible study and prayer. Some gather at work during their lunch hours for Bible study. There are no denominational or racial-ethnic boundaries. They discuss how they can be faithful followers in their work and in their homes. They are seeking and searching for a stronger faith that inspires them, carries them, and holds them when they are feeling lost. They hunger for a relationship with a loving God and seek out ways to make a difference in the world and in their community. They see lonely and depressed fellow workers, and so they reach out and are faithful and faith-filled.

Or imagine that the field trip to the aquarium is an intergenerational field trip with a church elder who shares with the children what the Jonah story meant to him while he was in the navy. Or imagine adults completing a Bible study and discussion on the church's website, which was designed by elementary children.

Such pictures of future possibilities are endless, but they must be uncovered. To do that we must have the freedom to dream and see with new eyes. There must be new pictures (the more the merrier) of the church's teaching ministry. Old models alone will not work as we enter a new century. We need to give up the image of full Sunday morning classrooms as being the only image for the teaching ministry of the church. Diane Hooge, an area minister in Massachusetts, has said, "We can remember the past, but we cannot reconstruct or relive it."

Biblical Message

We must expand our ministry and our vision of Christian education to include new models, and there are many exciting biblical messages about trying new things. Among those are:

(1)
O sing to the LORD a new song;
    sing to the LORD, all the earth! (Psalm 96:1, NRSV)

(2)
Do not remember the former things,
    or consider the things of old.
I am about to do a new thing;
    now it springs forth, do you not perceive it?
I will make a way in the wilderness
    and rivers in the desert. (Isaiah 43:18-19, NRSV)

(3)
I am about to create new heavens
    and a new earth;
the former things shall not be remembered
    or come to mind.
But be glad and rejoice forever
    in what I am creating. (Isaiah 65:17-18a, NRSV)

(4)
Neither is new wine put into old wineskins; otherwise, the skins burst, and the wine is spilled, and the skins are destroyed; but new wine is put into fresh wineskins, and so both are preserved. (Matthew 9:17, NRSV)

These passages encourage us to try new programs, but we must remember our ministry is to have faithful and faith-filled students. We must offer more than fluff, for that will only be fleeting. We must always remember that our goal is sharing the love of Jesus Christ and helping students discover the reality of that love in their hearts. *insert mission statement here*

As we begin to picture the future of our teaching ministry, let's keep two commandments in mind and put them into action:

(5)
You shall love the LORD your God with all your heart, and with all your soul, and with all your might. Keep these words that I am commanding you today in your heart. Recite them to your children and talk about them when you are at home and when you are away, when you lie down and when you rise. Bind them as a sign on your hand, fix them as an emblem on your forehead, and write them on the doorposts of your house and on your gates. (Deuteronomy 6:5-9, NRSV)

(6)
And Jesus added to this, "The second is this, 'You shall love your neighbor as yourself.' There is no other commandment greater than these." (Mark 12:31, NRSV)

The first commandment reminds us that faith comes first by loving God with our very being—our heart, soul, and might. Jesus then indicates that the second commandment to love our neighbor as ourselves is as great as the first. The Deuteronomy passage suggests that we are to be teaching all the time, everywhere—when we are lying down and rising up, at home and away. The message is to be bound on our hand, stamped on our foreheads, and fixed on the doorposts of our houses. It should be an integral part of us. The implication is that learning can happen all the time and in a wide variety of ways. We have to change the way we think. It is time for a new thing.

Some of us have no trouble picturing new programs or teaching methods, while others of us have a hard time letting go of past or current pictures of programs and methods. Doing a Bible study can help us with a biblical basis for picturing and trying new things. Two Bible study options are offered in shaded boxes.

20 min
2 8nd

Bible Study A

Materials Needed: Bibles
Time Needed: 45–60 minutes

Gather those involved in picturing the future of your teaching ministry.

Invite other interested persons.

Pray together, asking God for wisdom, discernment, eyes to see, and ears to hear.

Read the following Scriptures: Psalm 33:3; 96:1; 98:1; Isaiah 43:18-19; 65:17-18; 2 Corinthians 5:17; and Revelation 21:1-5.

Discuss: How do these Scriptures make you feel about being creative and picturing innovative programs? What do you think about the phrases, "Do not remember the former things" and "[Do not] consider the things of old" (NRSV)?

Read Mark 7:1-8.

Discuss: What does this passage tell you about sticking with tradition alone? What do you think the Pharisees were thinking? What was their goal? What was Jesus' reaction? What do you think Jesus cared about? What does verse 8 mean? How might it help you think about and picture the future of Christian education?

Bible Study B

Materials Needed: Bibles
Time Needed: 30–45 minutes

Read Matthew 9:16-17 (Mark 2:21-22; Luke 5:36-38).

Discuss: What are the "old wineskins" in our Christian education ministries? To what extent are they still working? To what degree are students growing in faith? Do participants look forward to coming to Christian education programs? What are our goals? What do we want to happen?

At this point you may wish to continue with the "creating new wineskins" exercise.

Can you picture a teaching ministry where Sunday school is not "Sunday school"? If not, please give yourself permission to dream and create. Teaching programs, worship, and ministries may happen anytime throughout the week. Worship may happen at 11:00 Sunday morning (or maybe not), but also at noon Tuesday, 7:00 Thursday night, and 5:00 Saturday night. There may be one program for six weeks in the fall and something different during Advent. Can you see this new picture with no, or a new, frame? Create new pictures and/or frames!

Pray that the "picturing the future" message is clear and led by those who are faithful and faith-filled. The goal is not increased numbers and cutesy programs, but programs that share the faith in inspiring ways. As we stand on the threshold of a new era, look and see the future, as Moses did! Be assured that it is one that is filled with children, youth, and adults who are faithful and faith-filled.

Creating New Wineskins
(an exercise in picturing new ways)

Materials Needed: Bible, newsprint, felt-tip markers
Time Needed: 45–60 minutes

Gather a group of people including teachers, members of the board or committee of Christian education, deacons, adults, youth, and older children.

Choose a recorder.

Pray together.

Distribute "Dream Dreams" permission slips (Reproducible Sheet 2) and indicate

that this is a time of sharing our ideas as wild as they might be, having fun and even getting silly, not evaluating.

Read the Bible story—Mark 4:35-41.

Listen to the story a second time. As you listen, imagine that you are in the boat with Jesus and the disciples.

Now imagine how many different ways you could teach this story. Brainstorm together your ideas, with the recorder listing them on newsprint. Remember, every idea gets recorded without the recorder editing them. Ideas are not to be debated but may be built upon.

Consider these questions after you've made an initial brainstorm list or if you get stuck: What senses did you experience in listening to this story? How can we use drama? Where? With whom? How can we use art? What kind of art? How can we use music? Where? When? How can we use computers? When? Where? Who? Who is teaching whom?

Go back through each line of the story and think through the action, thought, characters, and scene. What other ways of teaching this story come to mind now?

Notes

1. Liminality has been defined as a time in between one thing or another, a state betwixt and between (see Victor Turner, *The Ritual Process*, [Ithaca, N.Y.: Cornell University Presss, 1977]). It is when someone is at a crossroads, or at a threshold, ready to move from one stage to another.

2. "Deep Waters," a sermon by Daniel D. Chambers on February 8, 1998, at First Congregational Church of Berkeley.

Praying...
for Picturing the Future

- Enter into a time of prayer.
  Repeat this prayer,
  over and over,
  slowly and mindfully. Be still ...

God .... Grant me the
  Serenity to accept the things I cannot change...
  Courage to change the things I can...
  And the **Wisdom** to know the difference.
  Amen.

- Sing "Dreams and Visions."

Dreams and Visions

Words and Music by
Yohann Anderson

Embracing the Future: *A Guide for Reshaping Your Church's Teaching Ministry*

Learning...
for Picturing the Future

From others

Program Possibilities:

Sunday church school, Bible studies, books, new groups, seminars, intergenerational events, curriculum supplements, worship models, children's church, forum groups, video series, mission manias, service groups, church camps, day camps, adventure camps, vacation Bible school, retreats, support groups, youth fellowship groups, midweek groups, specialized groups, pastor's classes, mission trips, Lenten program, and parties

Some of these ideas are being discovered and tried by church groups and camps around the country. There is a wonderful comprehensive listing of Christian education models in "Christian Education Models" by S. Sue Amyx in *Blueprints for Building Christian Education*, Douglas D. Cripe, editor (St. Louis: Christian Board of Publication, 1997), 5–12. The author lists more than thirty models or programs included in the teaching ministry of the church, and no doubt even as you read this more ideas are being envisioned and tried out!

From the web

One of the newest and quickest ways to check out creative new ideas is to surf the web! Many of the things being tried by churches are those on the web. Check your own denominational web sites, link to churches who have home pages, and see what's happening inside their doors!

Some web sites to check out:

www.rotation.org—The official web site of the "Workshop Rotation Model" is an excellent site about a new model of Christian education. It lists churches involved in trying this model and has lesson plans for churches to try.

www.ecunet.org—Use this route to link with a number of different denominations and then to churches (of those denominations) with web pages. Check out what they are doing.

www.execpc.com/~chender—First Church of Cyberspace is creative, interesting, and has something for everybody. It is guaranteed to start discussions that could lead to many new ideas.

LEARNING

Sharing...
for Picturing the Future

It is important to educate the congregation and to communicate with them as you travel along the way on this new journey. The chances of success are better if you share with them the plans, dreams, struggles, and purpose. It is better to educate along the way rather than to spring something totally new on a congregation.

Through sermons, ministry moments in the worship service, intergenerational programs, suppers, small groups, newsletters, and special church mailings, update the congregation on the purpose and progress of your new ideas. Here are a few suggestions for helping others be ready for something new.

A Visual Time Line

Gather together such items as salt, rocks, fish, seeds, scrolls, older Bibles, older Sunday school curriculum materials, filmstrips, film projectors, movie reels, records, record players (they're probably all in a closet somewhere in the church), slides, eight-track tapes, cassette tapes, cassette recorders, videos, new curriculum materials, computer disks, a laptop computer, and a Bible on CD/ROM.

Use these items to make a visual time line displaying movement into a new century. These are all tools used by teachers to share the Good News! The time line shows that teachers have been using new tools all along. We need to remember that everything was new once. Use the Isaiah 43 or 65 or Revelation 21 passages as a caption. Add the name of a person or persons who may be contacted about the time line. Post the time line on a prominent bulletin board and let people know about it.

Moses Skit

Read Deuteronomy 34 as you prepare the skit and in worship (or at other events) before the skit is performed.

Have Moses climb to the top, tired, grumbling, complaining, and spending some time looking, wondering, and praying. Then have him "look" out (use binoculars or funny glasses) and "see" all the many possibilities of new ways to do ministries. A young person (representing Naphtali, which could be indicated by a sign placed on the young person's back) could approach or be seen trying something new. A child (representing Dan, which is indicated by a sign) could be shown trying something new. An adult (representing another place, perhaps your town or city with a sign indicating the same) could be shown trying something new or even dreaming up the new idea!

Pharisee Skit

Read Mark 7:1-8 as you prepare the skit and at the church event.

Prepare a skit based on the following and use it for a church-wide gathering. Have a group of Pharisees hanging around together complaining about Jesus' disciples not washing their hands. Try to make the "hand washing" issue sound really silly, trivial, and unimportant. When they approach Jesus, make sure his facial expressions and response are very clear. Try to leave this story in its historic context and let the message speak for itself. If you modernize it, do not let the Pharisees represent one particular age group or set of people and risk alienating anyone. The biblical message is clear on its own.

After each of these skits say a brief word or two about the planning group's work of picturing the future of your church's teaching ministry.

SHARING

Resources...
for Picturing the Future

Cripe, Douglas D., editor, *Blueprints for Building Christian Education,* (St. Louis: Christian Board of Publication, 1997). Two chapters of special note: "Christian Education Models" and "A Multitude of Media."

Foster, Charles R., *Educating Congregations: The Future of Christian Education,* (Nashville: Abingdon Press, 1994). Foster addresses the current concerns of traditional church school, leans toward "event-full" Christian education that has meaning for the participants and gives them hope.

Palmer, Parker J., *To Know As We Are Known: A Spirituality of Education,* (San Francisco: Harper & Row, 1993). Palmer helps Christian educators remember the importance of the spiritual dimension of teaching, getting away from a classroom setting that is only a time of information transformation and creating a space that builds upon openness, boundaries, and hospitality.

RESOURCES

Comment Sheet

We are eager to learn from users what has been helpful, has worked or not, or could have worked better, as well as what you have been able to accomplish with the help of this resource. Please take a few minutes to respond to the following questions and then send them to the address listed below. Use additional pages as needed.

1. These comments are in response to the following steps/chapters
    [please check the appropriate step(s) or chapter(s)]:
    ___ Seeing the Big Picture and Getting Started
    ___ Picturing the Future
    ___ Stating Our Mission
    ___ Assessing Our Situation
    ___ Shaping a Vision
    ___ Celebrating and Letting Go
    ___ Developing a Menu of Possibilities
    ___ Making an Action Plan

2. The most helpful part of this step in the planning process was . . .

3. The least helpful part of this step in the planning process was . . .

4. Changes you should consider are . . .

5. Consider adding the following resource(s) to the resource list:

6. Our key accomplishments related to this step of the planning process are . . .

7. Additional comments:

Thanks! Please return your comments to: Marcia Jessen, Educational Ministries, ABC/USA, P.O. Box 851, Valley Forge, PA 19482-0851; 610-768-2056 FAX; marcia.jessen@abc-usa.org

CHAPTER 3

Stating Our Mission

by David G. Berube

PURPOSE:

✓ discern and state your teaching mission

"Why do we need to provide 'education' anyway?" asked Kate. *"It seems to me that kids get educated all week at school. If we just share a Bible song and story and tell them how the church works, that's enough."*

"I'm glad you asked why we do this," said Imogene in her affirming way, "because that's a great place to begin deepening our look at our teaching ministry. If our church is going to provide the best possible teaching, we need to know why we're doing it."

❖

Whether you remember *Mission Impossible* as a television series or a Tom Cruise movie, you probably are familiar with the words "Your mission, should you decide to accept it. . . ."

If you remember the opening of the series, you'll remember that it had a patterned rhythm to it. Mr. Phelps, leader of the Impossible Mission Force (IMF), found a tape each week. The tape always began, "Good morning, Mr. Phelps. . . ." The recorded voice detailed a crisis that was threatening the very survival of the world as we know it, outlined the mission, and intoned the famous phrase.

Then the work began. The team assembled for a detailed briefing on the situation. The mission outline was expanded, the risk assessed, the objective stated and restated, and each person's role clearly understood and accepted. When the IMF team started out for Afghanistan or Zimbabwe or wherever, they set out with a detailed plan for where they were going, what they would do when they got there, and how they would know when the mission was accomplished. Because of the thoroughness of the plan, the team could even overcome unexpected problems and crises. Their good preparation allowed them to appropriately improvise when necessary.

The teaching mission of the church (perhaps *much* of the mission of the church) often presents a stark contrast to that. At some point, inspired by something, we, the traditional champions of the cause of propagating the gospel, attempt once again to whip ourselves and others into a mild fervor. "We've got to do something about the sorry state of Christian education in our church," we chant. At the exact moment inertia is overcome, or when we feel like it and have time, we mount our dead horses and drag them along, unsure where we're headed or what we'll do when we get there. Compared to the efficiency and effectiveness of Mr. Phelps and company, we look more like the crew of the SS Minnow.

Have no fear. This need not be a permanent condition. Our mission is not impossible. It is actually a guaranteed victory—if we're willing to connect with the One who makes it so and do what God needs. So, get the secret mini media disk from under your seat cushion, plug it into your "Teaching Mission Force" disk reader, and let's plan that "Mission Possible."

"Good morning, teaching mission planner . . ."

First, we need some common ground. Let's start with a definition of mission.

For the purpose of our work together, we'll use the following definition:

Mission is your overall reason for being, your purpose.

Your mission should be stated clearly and briefly, seeking to answer the question, "Why are we here?" A mission statement presents the big picture. It is the satellite image of the territory you operate within. Your mission is a long-term focal point for your ministry.

Next, we need to see that this mission is really *God's mission for you.* Whatever it winds up looking like in its parts and particulars, your teaching mission starts with the Lord. You discern it rather than determine it. This simple affirmation lifts up at least three important realities:

1. It raises the worth of your teaching mission. The mission is more than the desires and wants of a

Pontius' Puddle

HOWCUM' THAT BUSINESSES ARE WORKING UP MISSION STATEMENTS, WHILE CHURCH AGENCIES ARE MAKING BUSINESS PLANS?

Congregations may reprint this strip by noting its source and sending $10 to Joel Kauffmann, 111 Carter Road, Goshen, IN 46526.

group of Sunday school teachers. This ministry is beyond providing babysitting and games for the kids. This ministry, like all of the church's ministry, is from the Lord and for all people.

2. It clearly makes this *your* teaching mission. This is God's mission for **you**, in **your** place, in **your** time. Whatever your mission statement expresses, it needs to match the reality within which you find yourself. The mission statement, done well, avoids grandiose generalizations and disconnected plans that can't touch real lives.

3. It recognizes your teaching mission is part of something bigger. The mission is more than a program for the church. Your teaching mission is not just a "member only" opportunity. It extends beyond the walls of the church building and a formal membership list. Effective and faithful educational ministry crosses traditional boundaries and avoids compartmentalizing people. Jesus called us to go into the whole world with teaching. The specific focus of your particular church's teaching mission will cover considerably less territory than the whole world.

The point is that a mission statement ties our local mission to the broader mission of God.

Recognizing that our mission is God-given and serves the Lord's purposes for our specific ministry reminds us to use our gifts in meeting needs in our own situation and to follow the Lord. Given the importance of a mission statement, how do we go about discerning one?

"There is a need for a mission of teaching out there . . ."

If we assume (and I do) that life is more a journey we undertake than a course we complete, we need constantly to upgrade our experience. Throughout our lives we need the assistance that Christ gives through Scripture, worship, teaching, fellowship, and service. People need God's input all along the journey of life in order to make sense of reality and live meaningful lives. Consider some of the monumental reality shifts that face us currently and will continue (See Fig.1).[1]

These are not minor adjustments. They are major movements. While we won't address them specifically here, I offer them as an example of the world where we minister. Looking around closer to your church home, you will find them reflected in local reality.

Life is changing at a pace we have never known before, in ways that are chaotic and disorienting. Jesus was famous for stepping into the chaos of life, listening to the deepest needs of those present, and addressing them in specific ways that brought spiritual healing and order. Christ calls us to that same ministry in our day. We have a responsibility to get a clear picture of our field of ministry so we can be faithful.

"Your mission, should you decide to accept it . . ."

The key to determining the mission and doing the mission is a balance of good planning and committed action. Here is a plan for finding that balance. It will take about four hours in planning team sessions (4 one-hour sessions, 2 two-hour sessions, or a four-hour retreat). In addition you will want to spend time sharing with other church leaders and the decision-making group that must endorse the statement. The exact amount of time and number of sessions obviously will depend on your particular situation. The plan is accompanied by four shaded boxes giving detailed and timed outlines. You will note that there are three related reproducible sheets that may be used as masters for either handouts and/or overhead transparencies.

1. Gather the right team if you do not already have a team working on other steps in this plan. Enlist people

Shifting From	Shifting To
• Independent economies limited by national and political boundaries	• One global economy transcending political and national borders
• Focus on sports as primary leisure activity	• Focus on visual and performance arts
• Classical, Marxist Socialism of the collective	• "Capitalist Socialism" allowing individual entrepreneurship
• National and ethnic differences in lifestyles	• Homogenizing of world cultures (with an accompanying nationalist backlash)
• Government run welfare systems	• Privatized "workfare" systems
• Trade centered in Europe and North America	• Trade centered in the Pacific Rim nations
• Traditional, male-dominated business practices	• Innovative, female led business practices
• Understanding the world as a series of mechanical operations	• Understanding the world as the interaction of organic systems
• The dominance of science over religion	• The reemergence of significant religious belief (with the continuing decline of traditional mainline religious practice)
• The era of "The Movement," when groups influence change	• A new understanding of the importance of the individual in societal change
• An organized religion-based (U.S.) culture, where traditional religious affiliation is acceptable or at least benignly tolerated	• A secular culture that is at best suspicious of organized religion and, at worst, openly hostile toward it.

Figure 1

with a commitment to Christ and a passion for seeing the Christian life as one of continual growth in knowledge and experience with the Lord. Bring people onboard who see the teaching mission as an overall ministry of discipleship across the congregation and community, people who are unafraid to discover and try new ideas. Gather a team that includes a mix of the spiritual gifts of wisdom, exhortation, leadership, evangelism, administration, teaching, knowledge, and faith.[2] A good size is a team of five to eight people, at least a third of whom are new to the congregation in the last twelve to eighteen months.

2. Explore the Bible together. Two biblical texts stand out as powerful statements of the global mission and ministry of the body of Christ in the world.

The Greatest Commandment:

One of the scribes came near and heard them disputing with one another, and seeing that [Jesus] answered them well, he asked him, "Which commandment is the first of all?" Jesus answered, "The first is 'Hear, O Israel: the Lord our God, the Lord is one; you shall love the Lord your God with all your heart, and with all your soul, and with all your mind, and with all your strength.' The second is this,

'You shall love your neighbor as yourself.' There is no other commandment greater than these." (Mark 12:28-31, NRSV)

The Great Commission:

Jesus came and said to them, "All authority in heaven and on earth has been given to me. Go therefore and make disciples of all nations, baptizing them in the name of the Father and of the Son and of the Holy Spirit, and teaching them to obey everything that I have commanded you. And remember, I am with you always, to the end of the age." (Matthew 28:18-20, NRSV)

In the first text, Jesus points out that faith is expressed in love, demonstrated toward God and other people. In the second, he reminds us that the overall mission of Christians is to go to others, help them come to faith in God, and teach them the life lessons of the believer as Christ teaches us.

Reflect on how the global Christian mission impacts your local mission. What does it mean for you to be part of the wider body of Christ? How does your teaching mission relate to that global mission? Take time to reflect upon what it means for you to "go into the world," loving God and your neighbor as yourself.

Session 1

Materials Needed: Bibles, copies of Reproducible Sheets 3 and 4
Time Needed: 1 hour

A. A Time for Study and Prayer (20 minutes)

- Read together Mark 12:28-31.

- Engage the text using the questions on Reproducible Sheet 3.

- Pray, either led by one person or taking turns (see PRAYING for chapter 3).

B. An Introduction to Mission (10 minutes)

- The leader shares information from "Good morning, teaching mission planner" section of this chapter.

C. A Reintroduction to the World (20-30 minutes)

- The leader shares information from "There is a need for a mission of teaching out there" section of this chapter, guided by the questions on Reproducible Sheet 4.

3. Develop a provisional mission statement. As you pray and think about your local situation, what might your mission be? Who might it be with and for what reason? Why is that important? What are your team members passionate about in the realm of teaching ministry? As you begin to develop your mission statement, push yourself to look beyond what you've always done. The specific questions are less important than the intent—clarifying what the mission is, what it will entail to do it well, and whether or not the Lord equips you to do it.

When you write your statement, make it as clear as possible. A mission statement needs to be short enough to be memorable yet comprehensive enough to really mean something beyond a plan for next week. It must be broad enough to allow you room to grow yet specific enough to be manageable. It needs to point forward and be action oriented. This is a mobilization plan rather than a town charter. Here are some examples:

- Reaching others for God so they may reach toward God.

- We are a community of learners committed to the journey of faith and the spiritual growth of ourselves and others.

- We provide opportunities for learning about the Lord, ourselves, and others so that we will continue to be faithful followers of Christ.

- We call people to become followers of Jesus Christ and equip people to faithfully live out that call in the church and the world.

Session 2

Materials Needed: Bibles, copies of Reproducible Sheets 3 and 5, newsprint, felt-tip markers, and masking tape
Time Needed: 1 hour

A. A Time for Study and Prayer (20 minutes)

- Read together Matthew 18:18-20.

- Engage the text using the questions on Reproducible Sheet 3.

- Pray, either led by one person or taking turns (see **PRAYING** for chapter 3).

B. Developing a Provisional Mission Statement (40 minutes)

- The leader shares from the "Your mission, should you decide to accept it" section of chapter 3, on developing a provisional mission statement

- Reflecting upon the work done so far, the group answers the questions on Reproducible Sheet 5. Time is given to answer individually, then the whole group dialogs together, guided by the leader, with someone making notes on newsprint for the whole group to see.

- By the end of the session, the group should agree on a provisional statement. When you have a statement, ask yourselves these questions: Does this state an overall reason for being? Does it clearly state the purpose of our teaching mission? Does it clearly explain why we are here and what we are to do?

4. Try your statement out and get feedback. Run it past those you seek to reach, as well as leaders and members of your congregation. The response of those you seek to reach needs to carry a certain amount of extra weight. After all, if it doesn't work for them, it doesn't work. Testing it with leaders and congregational members helps see how it fits with the overall

mission of your church. Ask these questions of your reviewers: What do you hear this statement saying? How does that feel to you? How might you modify it so it could be more on target? Do very little to interpret the statement. If it needs interpretation, it probably still needs refining so it can communicate on its own. Check **SHARING** in this chapter for more ideas.

Session 3

Materials Needed: Bibles, copies of Reproducible Sheet 3, newsprint, felt-tip markers, and masking tape

Time Needed: 1 hour

A. A Time for Study and Prayer (20 minutes)

- Read together Mark 4:21-25.

- Engage the text using the questions on Reproducible Sheet 3.

- Pray, either led by one person or taking turns (see **PRAYING** for chapter 3).

B. Planning for Feedback from Others (40 minutes)

- Make a list of people to ask to review and respond to the provisional statement, and assign team members to contact them before the next session. Include people who are among the group you seek to reach. Limit the number to not more than two or three contacts per team member.

- Agree on questions to use (see "Your mission, should you decide to accept it" section of the chapter) from the following or from ones you develop:

  What do you hear this statement saying?

  How does that feel to you?

  What do you like about the statement?

  How might you modify it to make it clearer?

- Remind the group to make notes on the responses they get from the persons they contact so that the notes can be shared with the planning team.

5. Discuss the feedback and readjust as necessary. Avoid adjusting your statement simply because this is a new direction that doesn't fit the way things have always been done. Adjust for clarity based on what you heard from others.

Session 4

Materials Needed: Bibles, copies of Reproducible Sheet 3, newsprint, felt-tip markers, and masking tape

Time Needed: 1 hour

A. A Time for Study and Prayer (20 minutes)

- Read together Luke 1:26-38.

- Engage the text using the questions on Reproducible Sheet 3.

- Pray, either led by one person or taking turns (see **PRAYING** for chapter 3).

B. Checking in and Making Necessary Adjustments

- Share together reviewer comments on the provisional statement.

- Make any necessary adjustments to clarify the mission statement.

- Read the statement together and give thanks for the effort and results.

C. Identifying Next Steps (such as getting endorsement of your new teaching mission statement, having a congregational celebration of the new teaching mission statement, planning new ministry opportunity, or working on another step in this planning process [for instance, assessing your situation]). For detailed suggestions, see **SHARING** for chapter 3.

6. Get endorsement. The specific process of endorsement will vary by congregation. Whether it means a congregational vote, governing body approval, or some other mechanism, this step is very important. This is your congregation's teaching mission statement, not just your team's. For the statement to have integrity as your church's statement, the congregation needs to own it. See **SHARING** in this chapter for more ideas.

Undertake your mission

Once your team and congregation own your mission statement, pick a need in your local situation that matches your mission, develop a strategy for addressing it, gather the necessary resources, and try something—or continue with the other steps in this plan. If you plan a one-time experience, gather your team afterward to evaluate and reflect on how it went and how well it fit your mission. If it is a ministry of longer duration, check in along the way and evaluate it formally at regular intervals, at least every other month. Avoid overdoing evaluation, but evaluate. Without evaluation you can drift off your mission and not know it.

Developing a statement of your teaching mission may seem like an awful lot of work. It is. But when you consider that the option is to use limited resources and make blind stabs at ministry that miss more often than match needs, you will see that it is worth the effort. Stating our mission defines who we are (and who we are not) so that we can more effectively and faithfully serve Christ's ministry of discipleship for our world, our congregations, and ourselves.

"This message will self-destruct in five seconds . . ."
(Just kidding.)

Notes

1. John Naisbitt and Patricia Aburdene, *Megatrends 2000* (New York: William Morrow & Co., 1990), 13ff. Page 13 lists the trends, and each chapter is a discussion of a particular trend.

2. For a good discussion of these and other spiritual gifts, as well as a spiritual gifts inventory, see C. Peter Wagner, *Your Spiritual Gifts Can Help Your Church Grow* (Ventura, Calif.: Regal Books, 1994.) Also see Charles V. Bryant, *Rediscovering Our Spiritual Gifts* (Nashville: The Upper Room, 1996), and its accompanying workbook by John I. Penn.

Praying...
for Stating Our Mission

Use any or all of the following prayers or those of your own choosing.

A Prayer for Teachers

O God, you are the fountain of all truth; we ask you
to protect your church from all false teaching.
Protect the church
From all teaching and preaching which would
destroy people's faith;
From all that removes the old foundations without
putting anything in their place;
From all that confuses the simple,
that perplexes the seeker,
that bewilders wayfaring folks.
And yet at the same time protect the church
From the failure to face new truth;
From devotion to words and ideas which the passing
of the years has rendered
unintelligible;
From all intellectual cowardice and from all mental
lethargy and sloth.
O God, send to your church teachers,
Whose minds are wise with wisdom;
Whose hearts are warm with love;
Whose lips are eloquent with truth.
Send to your church teachers
Whose desire is to build and not to destroy;
Who are adventurous with the wise,
and yet gentle with the simple;
Who strenuously exercise the intellect,
and who yet remember that the heart has reasons of
its own.
Give to your church preachers and teachers who can
make known the Lord Christ to others because they
know him themselves; and give to your church hear-
ers, who, being freed from prejudice, will follow truth
as blind people long for light. This we ask through
Jesus Christ our Lord. Amen. [1]

Psalm 105:1-3 (NRSV)

O give thanks to the LORD, call on his name,
  make known his deeds among the peoples.
Sing to him, sing praises to him;
  tell of all his wonderful works.
Glory in his holy name;
  let the hearts of those who seek the LORD rejoice.

A Prayer in the Midst of Change

God grant me the serenity to accept the things
I cannot change;
Courage to change the things I can;
and Wisdom to know the difference;
Living one day at a time;
Enjoying one moment at a time;
Accepting hardships as the pathway to peace;
Taking, as He did, this sinful world as it is, not as I
would have it;
Trusting that He will make all things right if I surren-
der to His Will;
That I may be reasonably happy in this life and
supremely happy with Him forever in the next.
Amen.

A Prayer for Decision-Makers

O God, you know that our decisions affect the future.
Help us choose the right way.

Give us your guidance, and give us the humble obe-
dience to accept it.

Help us choose what you want, and others need,
rather than our own way.

Help us avoid decisions based on fear, or selfish-
ness, or sheer ease.

Help us today to ask humbly, "Lord, what would you
have us do?"

And wait for your answer and your leading.

Hear our prayer, and send an answer so clear that
we cannot mistake it. Amen. [2]

1. The prayer for St. Matthias Day (slightly adapted) from *A Barclay Prayer Book,* SCM Press and Trinity Press International 1990, pp 150f.

2. Based on William Barclay, *The Plainman's Book of Prayers* (London: Haper Collins Publishers Ltd.), 113-14.

Sharing...
for Stating Our Mission

- Additional ways of getting feedback on your pro visional mission statement:

  1. Share drafts with all church committees and/or all youth and adult church school classes and study groups. Have members of the planning team personally visit with each group, listening and making notes.

  2. Choose a random sample of church members with whom to share your provisional statement.

  3. Post copies of the provisional statement on prominent bulletin boards throughout the church building and ask for feedback. List planning team members and include a blank sheet of paper so responses can be made on the spot.

  4. Test out the provisional statement with representatives of any new groups of people you seek to reach. Go to where they are.

- Approaches for getting endorsement from the appropriate governing body in your church:

  1. Send copies of your statement to members of the group so they can become familiar with it ahead of the meeting.

  2. Have two or three members of the planning team introduce the mission statement and guide the conversation at the meeting.

- Ideas for celebrating and using your new teaching mission statement:

  1. Incorporate the statement into a litany to be used in corporate worship.

  2. Ask your pastor to preach a sermon based on the mission statement.

  3. Have a member of the planning team make a brief presentation about the statement in corporate worship.

  4. Have the gathered congregation read together the statement as a part of worship—perhaps for several Sundays in a row or on special teaching ministry Sundays, for example, Rally Day, Christian Education Sunday, Children's Day, Youth Sunday, Teacher Recognition Sunday.

  5. Invite someone to write a hymn or a new verse to an existing hymn based on the statement.

  6. Read the mission statement at the start of each meeting of your Christian education board, committee, or team.

SHARING

Resources...
for Stating Our Mission

Consider studying one or more of the resources listed here as you prepare to state the mission of your teaching ministry.

Books

Berkley, James D., editor, *Leadership Handbook of Outreach and Care,* (Grand Rapids: Baker, 1997). Part VI is specifically about Christian education. Each chapter, written by a different contributor, focuses on specific issues related to the church's teaching ministry. The topics are highlighted within the chapters by the use of helpful sidebars. Of particular help as you consider your teaching mission is chapter 22, "The Purpose of Christian Education." It gives a brief yet comprehensive sweep of the history of faith teaching philosophies and methods. It asks good questions that can focus a discussion of contemporary teaching mission and how it fits with the overall ministry of Christian teaching.

Cripe, Douglas D., editor, *Blueprints for Building Christian Education,* (St. Louis: Christian Board of Publication, 1997). Chapter 2, "Vision or Mission Statements," offers another process for discerning your teaching mission statement, as well as providing actual examples of church teaching mission statements. The chapter also lists and highlights other helpful resources on the teaching mission of the church.

Isham, Linda R., *Charting Our Course: Renewing the Church's Teaching Ministry,* (Valley Forge, PA: Judson Press, 1997). An excellent overall resource for understanding and examining your teaching mission. Chapter 2 speaks specifically of mission statements— their purpose, relationship to vision, and place within the whole ministry of the local church. The appendices offer valuable worksheets and checklists for developing a mission statement (pp. 57–61). Appendix G provides a resource list on teaching ministry.

Senge, Peter M., *The Fifth Discipline: The Art and Practice of the Learning Organization,* (New York: Currency Doubleday, 1994). This work comes from the world of business management and offers a new way of organizational life. Its organic approach is very consistent with the understanding of the church as the body of Christ. Its particular usefulness as you discern and implement your teaching mission comes in parts II, which explains what a learning organization is made of, and III, which outlines the disciplines that help a group become a learning organization. As you begin to think in new ways, this resource provides a valuable framework to assist the transition.

Periodicals

Leadership is "A Practical Journal for Church Leaders" published quarterly by Christianity Today, Inc., 465 Gundersen Drive, Carol Stream, IL 60188-2498. Articles deal with an array of church leadership issues, although many of the insights will prove helpful within the teaching ministry of a local church. You may view a sample of the current issue online at **www.christianity.net/leadership.**

Net Results is a monthly resource of practical articles on various church topics, including teaching ministry. It is distributed by Cokesbury, 1-800-672-1789. Their Internet home page is **www.llano.net/net-results**.

Internet Resources

www.cforc.com offers a self-administered "Spiritual Gifts Discovery Tool" that can be taken on- or offline. The survey involves reacting to each of 110 statements on a scale of 4 (strongly agree) to 0 (completely disagree). From your responses a ranking of your gifts is created, which can help direct you toward ministries for which you are gifted. The site also has a "List of Gifts" for further study of your gifts. It takes only about fifteen minutes to complete and presents spiritual gifts in a practical ministry way.

www.easum.com is the home page for 21st Century Strategies. This ministry seeks to help churches continue to minister in vital ways in the midst of contemporary cultural realities. Among a vast array of resources, including consultation services, e-mail forums, videos, and seminars, I recommend highly the book *Sacred Cows Make Gourmet Burgers.* This work by William Easum is an honest, comprehensive look at contemporary culture and the church. It provides a springboard and tools for looking at how faithful ministry will happen for the present and future. It also has tremendous bibliographic resources.

Comment Sheet

We are eager to learn from users what has been helpful, has worked or not, or could have worked better, as well as what you have been able to accomplish with the help of this resource. Please take a few minutes to respond to the following questions and then send them to the address listed below. Use additional pages as needed.

1. These comments are in response to the following steps/chapters
    [please check the appropriate step(s) or chapter(s)]:
    ___ Seeing the Big Picture and Getting Started
    ___ Picturing the Future
    ___ Stating Our Mission
    ___ Assessing Our Situation
    ___ Shaping a Vision
    ___ Celebrating and Letting Go
    ___ Developing a Menu of Possibilities
    ___ Making an Action Plan

2. The most helpful part of this step in the planning process was . . .

3. The least helpful part of this step in the planning process was . . .

4. Changes you should consider are . . .

5. Consider adding the following resource(s) to the resource list:

6. Our key accomplishments related to this step of the planning process are . . .

7. Additional comments:

Thanks! Please return your comments to: Marcia Jessen, Educational Ministries, ABC/USA, P.O. Box 851, Valley Forge, PA 19482-0851; 610-768-2056 FAX; marcia.jessen@abc-usa.org

Assessing Our Situation

by Beth Keating

"I understand that there used to be men's and women's classes, too," offered Art, "but we don't do that anymore. Nor do we have a youth group, or a young married's, or a widow's meeting. We're just a small church."

"Maybe those groups don't meet anymore, Art," Imogene said, "But there are new groups in our community who, I think we'll all agree, could benefit from experiencing and growing in their faith . . ."

O ne of our family rituals is the summer vacation. It involves packing the car to its limit, settling our two children in the back seat with games, crackers, and gum, as my husband and I climb into the front seats. My husband usually drives while I navigate (that means I hold the map open on my lap). My work requires that I drive hundreds of miles a week, so it is a joy to sit in the passenger seat and see the world, in living color and minute detail, as we pass through it. This is such a joy for me that I frequently become completely caught up in the world outside the car, forgetting both the map on my lap and my task to keep us on the right road, headed in the right direction. When we suddenly realize that we are not where we are supposed to be, I feverishly begin looking at the map, not to see where we came from or where we are going (I usually have that pretty well figured out) but where on that page our car is right at that moment. Unless I know where we are, I'll never be able to help us reach our destination.

You may have guessed that this is not an uncommon occurrence for our family, rather it has become part of our summer vacation ritual. When I am the navigator, the question often is, "But where are we now?"

"But where are we now?" is a significant question to consider as we work through this planning process.

When exercising, improper use of muscles not yet strengthened and toned may result in injury or lead to discouragement. As in exercising, it is important to know what shape we are in and where we are before we make plans that will strengthen our teaching ministry. This chapter will suggest thoughts for consideration and resources to help assess our situation so that we have a basis for affirming current or determining new directions for our ministry. Many resources are available to churches as they consider evaluating their current ministry (see **RESOURCES** for this chapter).

As you read through this chapter, you will find that our study will consider three areas: the church, the teaching ministry, and the world. You may recognize that your church has already spent significant time looking at one or more of these areas and you have sufficient data to help you form a picture of where your congregation is as it relates to the church, the teaching ministry, or the world. Exercises are provided to guide you through a process of self-study in each area. These are found in shaded boxes in this chapter. Feel free to use any or all of them as you assess your current ministry. The first shaded boxes (Church Shield) should be started as you assess your church and is designed to be built upon in successive exercises.

Church Shield

Materials Needed: large sheet of newsprint, felt-tip markers, masking tape

Design a large shield, or coat of arms, that will be a visible expression of where your church sees itself now. On a large sheet of newsprint, draw the outline of your coat of arms (see illustration).

Draw a cross in the center. In the top left-hand corner, draw a picture of your church. Display this drawing where it is visible to the planning group. You will be adding to each section of the shield as you work through the exercises that follow.

Drawing of your church here

The Church

This aspect of assessing where you are focuses on the identity of your church. In the *Handbook for Congregational Studies,* Carroll, Dudley, and McKinney define identity as "that persistent set of beliefs, values, patterns, symbols, stories and style that make a congregation distinctively itself."[1]

Some of what shapes the church's identity is defined by the denomination to which it belongs. Certain denominational characteristics (mode of baptism, understanding of the Eucharist or Communion, style of church government, basic theological understandings, mission understanding and emphasis) form the basic identity and define the church's theology. Within the context of any denomination there is room, however, for a church to define its own personality and identity. Worship style, social awareness, outreach, and ministry emphases are some of the ways in which a church may define itself in the context of a wider church family.

It is important to understand who your church is within the congregation, within the denomination, and in the community. Studying the "set of beliefs, values, patterns, symbols, stories, and style" as perceived from people within the congregation and from others who are outside will help you understand who you are as a church. If your church has recently done a self-study for the purpose of long-range planning or to prepare for calling a new pastor, your work in this area has been completed for you and you will simply need to review the information that has been gathered. If not, you will want to take some time to consider what it means to be part of the family of faith in your church. Reproducible Sheet 6 lists topics and related study questions that will help you form a picture of who you are as a church.

Gathering and Analyzing Data

Materials Needed: copies of Reproducible Sheet 6, the church shield, newsprint, felt-tip markers, masking tape
Time Needed: 1½–2 hours

Before meeting assign one of the four following topics: statistical information, beliefs, rituals, and symbols to members of the committee. Have each person collect data and bring it to the meeting. The information that deals with numerical data can be gathered from facts that are kept in the church office, by the Sunday school superintendent, or by the pastor. The other information is best collected by talking with one another, meeting in small groups, interviewing selected persons in the congregation, and talking with new persons who have recently come into the congregation.

1. Spend an hour reporting in on information that was gathered. Give opportunity for each person to share her or his own perceptions. Record significant observations on newsprint.

2. Spend ½ to 1 hour as a group, working through #5 on Reproducible Sheet 6 using information that was gathered and shared. Work together to write a statement that best represents the character and personality of your church.

3. Design a symbol for the church shield and add it to the upper right corner.

This statement of your church's identity and the picture added to the shield become the first step in discovering where you are now.

The Teaching Ministry

The second step involves assessing your current Christian education ministry. This will involve developing an understanding of the church's Christian education priorities, assessment of staff, and looking at current classes/learning opportunities available to find areas of strength and possibilities for growth. The assessment tool (Reproducible Sheet 7) could be completed by members of the board of Christian education, education committee, teaching ministry team, and/or members of the congregation. If you share it with the larger congregation, build into your group sharing time to gather in this information from the wider congregation.

The World

The final area that needs to be considered as a church assesses its current teaching ministry is the world outside the walls of the church. In *Effective Church Leadership,* Kennon Callahan writes, "The day of the unchurched culture is over. The day of the mission church has come."[2] In *Twelve Keys to an Effective Church,* he writes, "The dark malaise of the Christian church in our time is that so many congregations have developed a preoccupation with their weaknesses, their problems, and their concerns. It is as if there were no open tomb or risen Lord. It is as if these congregations preferred to live locked in a closed tomb, focusing on their past and refusing to recognize the strengths God has shared with them that they might be in mission in this world."[3]

An assessment of the world should be done on two levels. First, a demographic study of your community will help you envision your mission field. Some statistical demographic information is available from the United States Census Bureau. Most denominations also now subscribe to demographic information that includes the number of persons in the community in each age group, average incomes, professional information, religious preferences, areas of rapid growth, and so forth. Check with your denomination's regional or national office (listed in Denominational Contact Information at the end of this resource) for information on how to order a demographic study of your community.

Demographic information on communities is also now available on the Internet. If you do not have access to the Internet on your computer, a visit to your local library and assistance from the librarian will quickly put you in touch with demographic information available online.

Second, prayerful consideration should be given to the specific social, economic, and spiritual needs of your community. What are the issues and concerns of your community? What makes the headlines in your local paper? Who are the oppressed in your community and in the world? What are some specific ways your church is addressing the social concerns of your community? As you meet to strategize strengthening your teaching ministry, build in time to consider how you are called to minister in your community. The **PRAYING** and **LEARNING** resources of this chapter can help guide you through this process. This might best be accomplished by discussing these questions in a number of small groups in your church. A response could be drafted by combining notes taken in each small group.

the group mark (using self-adhesive dots or a variety of colored markers) those areas of greatest concern in the community and world.

3. Design a final picture or symbol that best represents your church's role in ministry to the community and world. Add this picture to the lower right corner of your church shield.

Conclusion

If you have followed the steps in this chapter, you should now have a clear picture of who you are as a church, how you are currently carrying out your teaching ministry, and those to whom you have been called to minister. The shield you have drawn is a symbolic representation of how you see yourselves, your mission, and your teaching ministry. Share your shield with the wider church family. Celebrate together the strengths and gifts, the ministry and opportunities for ministry with which God has blessed your congregation. You may want to write a litany of thanksgiving and praise to the God who calls you to share in ministry.

By now you know where you are! As you move ahead, you will get a clearer picture of where God is calling you to be!

Notes

1. Jackson W. Carroll, Carl S. Dudley, and William McKinney, eds., *Handbook for Congregational Studies* (Nashville: Abingdon Press, 1986), 12.

2. Callahan, Kennon, *Effective Church Leadership* (San Francisco: Harper & Row, 1990), 13.

3. Callahan, Kennon, *Twelve Keys to an Effective Church* (San Francisco: HarperSanFrancisco, 1983), xxi.

Praying...
for Assessing Our Situation

Enter into prayer
 with grateful hearts
 as listeners
  seeking to discern God's vision for the
  teaching ministry of your church, present
  and future.

"Extend your arms in welcome to the future. The best is yet to come."

          - Anthony de Mello[1]

"I pray that the God of our Lord Jesus Christ, the Father of glory, may give you a spirit of wisdom and revelation as you come to know him, so that, with the eyes of your heart enlightened, you may know what is the hope to which he has called you, what are the riches of his glorious inheritance among the saints, and what is the immeasurable greatness of his power for us who believe, according to the working of his great power."

         Ephesians 1:17-19, NRSV

- **Celebrate** together the history and tradition with which God has blessed your congregation. Specifically name and thank God for strengths and gifts that are seen among God's people in your fellowship.

In a circle prayer have participants name gifts, programs, classes, teachers, and so forth that bring energy, strength, and power to your teaching ministry. After each is named, have the whole group respond with a refrain, such as, "Thank you Lord, for your gifts of grace."

- **Meditate** and wait for the Lord to reveal those areas of your teaching ministry that need to be strengthened. Consider the needs of each of the areas named in the chapter: the church, the teaching ministry, and the world.

"Prayer is the way to both the heart of God and the heart of the world—precisely because they have been joined through the sufferings of Jesus Christ.... Praying is letting one's own heart become the place where the tears of God and the tears of God's children can merge and become tears of hope."[2]

In circle prayer have participants name concerns, areas of need, and visions that grow out of compassion. After each is named, have the whole group respond with a refrain, such as, "Thank you God, for giving us vision."

- **Affirm** the ministry that is now yours and that to which you feel you might be called.

Sing or recite together "We Are God's People"

- **Pray** the following poem.

Prayer for a Questioning Heart

It seems to me Lord
that we search
much too desperately
for answers
when a good question
holds as much grace
as an answer.

Jesus
you are the Great Questioner.
Keep your questions alive
that we may always be seekers
rather than settlers.

Guard us well
from the sin of settling in
with our answers
hugged to our breasts.

Make of us
 a wondering
 far-sighted
 questioning
 restless people
And give us the feet of pilgrims
on this journey unfinished.[3]

1. Anthony de Mello, *Wellsprings* (Garden City, N.Y.: Image Books, 1986), 239.
2. Henri Nouwen, *Seeds of Hope,* Robert Durback, ed. (New York: Bantam Books, 1989), 68.
3. "Prayer for a Questioning Heart" from *Seasons of Your Heart: Prayers and Reflections* by Macrina Wiederkehr. Copyright © 1991 by Macrina Wiederkehr. Reprinted by permission of Harper Collins Publishers, Inc.

We Are God's People

Bryan Jeffery Leech, 1976

Johannes Brahms, 1877
arr. Fred Bock, 1976

Learning...
for Assessing Our Situation

Enter into study
    with open minds and hearts
    as teachers
        and
    students

The Song of the Seed

Suddenly I am a child again
Awakening from a deep sleep,
trusting a hand
held out in the darkness
inviting me to rise and live.

Suddenly I am a child again
Allowing eternal questions
to rise in my soul,
asking the questions aloud, aloud
in silence, in silence, in silence,
and finally a silence that is loud.
No longer afraid
to seek the mystery, questioning.
No longer afraid of eternal questions.

Suddenly I am not afraid of what I do not know
Unafraid of what I do not understand
Suddenly I am delighted
to take the hand of an unseen God,
leading me through a comforting darkness
in which I do not see the stars
but feel them rising in my heart.

Suddenly I am a child
unashamed and unafraid
to reach out in the darkness for a hand.

Suddenly I am an awakened child. [1]

- Read about and discuss the history of your congregation. What have been the areas of greatest strength in ministry? For what has your church been known in your community and in your denomination?

- Read Ephesians 4:1-16 and list gifts that you see among people in your congregation. Lead a study on spiritual gifts. Help church members assess their gifts and find ways to use them in ministry. An excellent resource is *Discover Your Gifts* by Alvin J. Vander Griend. See **RESOURCES** for this chapter.

- Share together in the following spiritual exercise. Find a comfortable position, relax, and allow the Spirit to guide your thoughts as someone reads the following words.

1. "The Song of the Seed" from *The Song of the Seed* by Macrina Wiederkehr. Copyright © 1995 by Macrina Wiederkehr. Reprinted by permission of Harper Collins Publishers, Inc.

I recall the words of Paul,
"Let this mind be in you
which was in Christ Jesus."

I ask the Lord to offer me his heart.
I see him take away my heart of stone,
put in its place his heart of flesh.

I feel the strange sensation
of returning to my world
with someone else's heart.

I walk along a busy street
the street outside our church.
The usual crowds are everywhere
and I look at them, to my astonishment,
in a strangely different kind of way today.
The sight of them awakens thoughts and
    feelings
quite different from the ones I am accus-
    tomed to.

I see the faces of persons as they pass by
and see loneliness
emptiness
hunger
fear
pain.

I see people wandering
like sheep without a shepherd
and in my heart
the heart of Christ
I am filled with compassion.

I notice that with this new heart of mine
there are occasions
when my heart dissolves in tenderness
and others when it burns with indignation.

I allow the Spirit to sow within me
seeds
of love for those who are unloved
of justice for those who are beaten down
of peace for those who are confused
of hope for those who cannot bear to see
    tomorrow
of joy for the joyless.

I stop
and look in the faces.
I wait for the Spirit to direct me
to direct us
to fill us with a vision
for his kingdom . . . in this place.

I set out for my home
and as I walk I look at trees and birds,
at clouds and animals and all of nature
with a different kind of vision
with hope for the future
and joy in the presence of the Spirit.

Sharing...
for Assessing Our Situation

SHARING

Be prepared to share with the larger congregation your assessment of where you see your church, its teaching ministry, the world.

Remember in your work together that you are part of a larger community. "Community is an outward and visible sign of an inward and invisible grace, the flowing of personal identity and integrity into the world of relationships."[1]

- Report regularly to the congregation as you begin to form a picture of your assessment of your congregation and its teaching ministry.

- Post newsprint "graffiti sheets" for persons to write their comments, observations, and assessments as you look at each of the three areas of study: the church, the teaching ministry, the world.

- Ask your pastor to preach a sermon series on spiritual gifts and encourage each person to discover his/her own gift. Compile and post a list of gifts and have persons add their name to the appropriate place on the list.

- Post the church shield that you are working on and call attention to each of the sections, explaining in your newsletter, on a Sunday morning, and at church council meetings the meaning of the symbols. Encourage feedback from members of the congregation.

- Invite the youth to become involved by sharing with you the needs and concerns of youth in your community. Ask them how the church might respond to those needs.

- Invite church members to pray for your church, your teaching ministry, the community, and the world.

1. Parker J. Palmer, *The Courage to Teach* (San Francisco: Jossey-Bass, 1998), 90.

Resources...

for Assessing Our Situation

Callahan, Kennon L., *Effective Church Leadership*, (San Francisco: Jossey-Bass, 1997). Building on *The Twelve Keys*, this book relates to leadership style in a mission-oriented church.

Callahan, Kennon L., *Twelve Keys to an Effective Church*, (San Francisco: Jossey-Bass, 1997). Uses a planning process based on ministering from the strengths of the church and responding to the passion for ministry.

Carroll, Jackson W., Carl S. Dudley, and William McKinney, editors, *Handbook for Congregational Studies,* (Nashville: Abingdon Press, 1986). Written by participants in the Project Team for Congregational Studies, an informal partnership of representatives from the Alban Institute, Auburn Theological Seminary, Candler School of Theology, Hartford Seminary, McCormick Theological Seminary, and the research offices of the Presbyterian Church (U.S.A.) and the United Church Board for Homeland Ministries, this is an excellent book filled with resources on assessing and understanding your local church.

Carroll, Jackson W., Carl S. Dudley, Nancy Ammerman, and William McKinney, editors, *Studying Congregations,* (Nashville: Abingdon Press, 1998). A new edition of Handbook for Congregational Studies.

Harris, Maria, *Fashion Me A People: Curriculum in the Church,* (Louisville: Westminster John Knox, 1989). A thoughtful presentation of the curriculum as it relates to the whole church experience.

Isham, Linda R., *Charting Our Course: Renewing the Church's Teaching Ministry,* (Valley Forge, PA: Judson Press, 1997). A careful leading through the wilderness of the current times in which we live. Provides resources for study and suggestions for implementation.

Palmer, Parker J., *The Courage to Teach: Exploring the Inner Landscape of a Teacher's Life,* (San Francisco: Jossey-Bass, 1998). "This book builds on a simple premise: good teaching cannot be reduced to technique; good teaching comes from the identity and integrity of the teacher."

Vander Griend, Alvin J., *Discover Your Gifts,* (Grand Rapids: Church Development Resources, A Ministry of CRC Publication, 1996). A good resource for studying spiritual gifts; includes an inventory for persons seeking to find their spiritual gift.

RESOURCES

Comment Sheet

We are eager to learn from users what has been helpful, has worked or not, or could have worked better, as well as what you have been able to accomplish with the help of this resource. Please take a few minutes to respond to the following questions and then send them to the address listed below. Use additional pages as needed.

1. These comments are in response to the following steps/chapters [please check the appropriate step(s) or chapter(s)]:

___ Seeing the Big Picture and Getting Started
___ Picturing the Future
___ Stating Our Mission
___ Assessing Our Situation
___ Shaping a Vision
___ Celebrating and Letting Go
___ Developing a Menu of Possibilities
___ Making an Action Plan

2. The most helpful part of this step in the planning process was . . .

3. The least helpful part of this step in the planning process was . . .

4. Changes you should consider are . . .

5. Consider adding the following resource(s) to the resource list:

6. Our key accomplishments related to this step of the planning process are . . .

7. Additional comments:

Thanks! Please return your comments to: Marcia Jessen, Educational Ministries, ABC/USA, P.O. Box 851, Valley Forge, PA 19482-0851; 610-768-2056 FAX; marcia.jessen@abc-usa.org

CHAPTER 5

Shaping a Vision

by Linda R. Isham

PURPOSE:

 describe vision

 explore criteria for a vision statement

 consider an example church's vision statement

outline a process for developing a vision statement

"It's overwhelming to me as I sit here thinking about all the things we could do. I can easily see us doing nothing well because we're trying to do too much," shared Pastor Pat.

"I agree." Imogene said sincerely, "That's why it's important that we're clear about what God wants us to accomplish in the next, smaller piece of the future."

An oft-quoted phrase, "Without vision the people perish," is equally adapted to the church and its teaching ministry. Without vision the church's teaching ministry perishes or at best languishes. In many churches today we have lost vision, indeed, lost our courage and heart for the teaching ministry.

What is required is shaping, reshaping, or renewing a vision for our church's teaching ministry. First, we must reclaim our corporate courage and heart for the teaching ministry. Shaping a vision requires a deep commitment to and passion for teaching. We come to new or renewed vision for the teaching ministry from a strong conviction that teaching is central to the ministry and mission of the church today. We come believing that we must pass on what we ourselves know—that Jesus Christ is Lord and Savior and that we as Christians and the church are called to be a transforming presence in the world. We come believing that the world is seeking to know this Good News but does not always hear because of the ways we teach. We come believing that the community of believers called the church can and must teach and learn.

How then do we go about reclaiming a heart for teaching? We find the one or two persons who have such a heart and invite them to share their testimonies. We talk with church members about our own heart for teaching. We ask for sermons on teaching. We talk with other churches about our desire to reclaim a heart for teaching. We have conversations, read books, view videos, and join electronic meetings that can spark such a fire in our hearts for teaching. We tell our stories.

Such reclamation does not happen overnight, and even as we are seeking such a heart we can begin the work of shaping a vision for our teaching ministry. Who knows—maybe we'll find our heart and courage for teaching as we shape the vision!

Describing Vision

Let's review what a vision statement is, particularly in relationship to a mission statement. A vision statement is future-oriented. It speaks about how we'll look and what we'll do. It is hopeful and filled with promise. It comes from spending time in discerning what God would have us be and do as a teaching church.

A vision statement grows from and gives legs to the mission statement, which describes the reason we exist. Those legs can and should be changed or modified from time to time. A vision statement, while focusing on the future, can help us keep from focusing on the past and the way we've always done things. It becomes a bridge from the past into the future.

A vision statement doesn't get into the details and specifics of how, who, what, when, and where. It is more global in the way in which it speaks about what and how we'll do the teaching ministry in the future.

Considering Criteria

Two verses from Habakkuk point us toward some criteria: "Write the vision; make it plain on tablets, so that a runner may read it. For there is still a vision for the appointed time" (Habakkuk 2:2b-3a, NRSV). There are four criteria to keep in mind when writing vision statements:

1. Describe the vision in terms of the future.

2. State it clearly and in a compelling way (so that someone who did not write it can understand and commit himself or herself to it).

3. Use vivid language and make it motivational.

4. Keep it short.

Let's test the criteria on a couple of examples of vision statements from areas other than the church and Christian education.

A man on the moon by the end of the decade. (John F. Kennedy)

A personal computer in every home that everyone can use. (Bill Gates)

You might think of other examples of vision statements. To what extent do these two vision statements, and any you add, meet the criteria?

Enter Old New Century Church

Old New Century Church found itself facing several challenges in the area of its teaching ministry and decided to take a good look at what it would like to be doing in the future, review the purpose for its teaching ministry, and assess its current teaching ministry. The teaching ministry team agreed to take on the responsibility for this planning work.

In their first session each person was asked to draw a picture of what he or she thought their teaching ministry would look like in 2004. These were then shared within the group and later posted on a bulletin board in a prominent place in the church building. They asked for others to draw pictures of what they thought the teaching ministry of Old New Century Church would look like in 2004. They received pictures from children, youth, and adults of all ages. After viewing them, the pictures were posted on the bulletin board for all to see. There was much conversation, for many images had surfaced— from a computer-equipped resource room, to intergenerational Advent, Lent, and Pentecost programs out in the community, to Sunday mornings off for church school teachers to go to training seminars and other teacher Sabbath programs, to people of all ages involved in interactive, life-application Bible study at many different times and places.

In another session the teaching ministry team reviewed the purpose of their teaching ministry, revised it slightly, and shared this with the entire congregation in the form of a litany in morning worship: We call people to become followers of Jesus Christ and equip people to faithfully live out that call in the church and in the world.

After some assessment of their current situation and taking another look at their future pictures, they decided to spend an evening working on a vision for the future. Their work (after a little editing by one of the team members!) resulted in the following statement:

Give attention to those not now part of our faith community;

Reclaim our courage and heart for teaching the faith;

Orchestrate ways for people to learn to be a transforming presence in the world;

Walk with those we call to lead and teach others.

Getting Ready

As you plan to work on shaping a vision for the future of your church's teaching ministry, there are several things you need to determine. Who will be the responsible group? Who will guide the process? Who else will you involve beside the initiating group (see **SHARING** at the end of this chapter for ideas)? How much time will you need and when and where will you do this? If you already have a mission statement, have done some assessing of your situation, and have some pictures of the future, have those pieces ready to inform your work.

This step, outlined in the Shaping a Vision shaded box, takes approximately four hours to complete. It may be done in one session or two 2-hour sessions. A good breaking point is between steps 7 and 8. As you begin step 8, you will have approximately two hours of work remaining, so time yourselves accordingly.

The process assumes that the group involved is the body in your church responsible for Christian education. In preparation for this session(s) post the purpose of this session on newsprint or a chalkboard for all to see. Check the refrain pages for this chapter for ideas on praying, learning, and sharing. Pause whenever the Spirit moves you to pray for discernment and guidance and/or to offer prayers of gratitude. Encourage everyone to contribute and be heard.

Shaping a Vision

Materials Needed: newsprint, felt-tip markers, masking tape, and/or overhead projector and transparencies, Bibles, self-adhesive colored dots (available from an office supply store), Reproducible Sheet 8
Time Needed: approximately 4 hours in one session or two 2-hour sessions

1. Review the purpose of the session(s): to shape a vision for our church's teaching ministry in a new century.

2. Working as a total group or in smaller groups, respond to each of the following

open-ended statements, recording responses on newsprint for all to see.

"What first interested me, and/or continues to excite me, about the teaching ministry of our congregation is. . . ."

"What disappoints me about the teaching ministry of our congregation is. . . ."

If working in small groups, ask each group to be prepared to share these with the larger group.

3. Pause to give thanks to God for all the interesting and exciting things about the teaching ministry of your congregation and ask God's help in recognizing and letting go of those things that disappoint you about your church's teaching ministry.

4. Explore Scripture passages for clues about what might transform the church's teaching ministry and guide you in shaping a vision for the future. Look for key words and phrases that suggest the ingredients of God's vision for your teaching ministry. Divide into pairs and assign each pair one or more of the following Scripture passages (or passages of your choosing) and questions. Ask the pairs to share their findings with the group.

   • Deuteronomy 6:4-9

   What actions are commanded?

   How might similar actions look if carried out today?

   • Exodus 13:14-16

   What teaching model is described in this brief account?

   How might the model be employed in today's teaching?

   • Matthew 28:18-20

   By what authority is the church commissioned to teach?

   • Ephesians 4:11-16

   What does this passage imply about the relationship between teaching and other ministries of the church?

   • Luke 10:25-37

   What are the key teaching methods that Jesus used?

   How might Jesus' message and methods as shown in this passage be used today?

5. Note that the passages deal with a variety of concerns related to the teaching ministry—actions, models, authority, relationship with other ministries, methods, and message. As you hear reports, record on newsprint key words and phrases under the heading "Biblical Insights."

6. Share ideas about the meaning of vision, using information from this chapter and Reproducible Sheet 8.

7. If you have information from the assessing our situation step, post it under the heading "Christian Education Needs Today." If you have not done that step, identify now teaching ministry needs and concerns in the congregation and the community, recording these on newsprint under the heading "Christian Education Needs Today."

8. Take a break while one or two people arrange the following newsprint lists in front of the group: "What Interests and Excites Us," "Biblical Insights," and "Christian Education Needs Today."

9. Following the break, have each person choose from the posted lists five (you might choose a number more or less, depending on the size of your lists, the size of your congregation, and your own preferences) things he or she believes most need to be part of this church's vision for its future teaching ministry. Give all participants a felt-tip marker or five self-adhesive colored dots and have them mark their five choices. Indicate that you are seeking to find those areas perceived as most important to this group, and when done with this step, you will have components of an initial vision statement.

10. Tally the results. Note the five items with the most votes. Discuss, analyze, and combine items as appropriate.

11. Review the top five (or however many) items. Spend five minutes recording signs/actions/ideas for each of the vision components so that the components can be filled out a bit and the group can begin to build ownership for them. Remind the group that every idea gets recorded and that now is not the time for debate. That comes later. Set a timer if it will help keep the process moving. Indicate that this is to be a creative process and the permission meter is as high as it can go—on a scale of 1 to 10, it's on 10!

12. Refine the work from the previous step, dividing up your time so that not all of the time is spent on one component. Use the lists to guide you in drafting a vision statement or components of a statement. Record your work on newsprint, and if you work in small groups, share in the total group.

13. Post, report, and discuss your work. Give yourselves a round of applause or a pat on the back! Offer prayers of thanksgiving for good work.

14. Determine with whom you'll share your vision statement draft for comments and who will take the draft and comments and prepare a second or final draft. See this chapter's SHARING.

Praying...
for Shaping a Vision

Enter into prayer
> with an open mind,
> with hearts of hope
> > focusing on the future.

Remember the words of Susan Muto: "To pray without ceasing is to thank God for promises fulfilled and hopes for what the future holds."

Invite the congregation to be in prayer with you, to join you as prayer partners.

Use any or all of the following prayer resources or those from your own rich storehouse.

- Sing or read the words to stanzas 1 and 2 of the hymn "Be Thou My Vision" as a prayer. Consider changing the singular pronouns to plural—"my" to "our," for example.

- Focus your praying for vision in the following ways—guided, in silence or out loud:

    Pray for . . .

    a dream to be seen,
    a call to be heard,
    a passion for our hearts,
    a hope to be voiced,
    projects and programs for our hands,
    and
    maps for our feet.

- Ask individuals to express how they need to be equipped for shaping a vision for the church's teaching ministry. After each person's request, the group responds with the phrase: "Be thou our vision, O Lord of our hearts." Close with everyone in unison repeating the phrase: "Be thou our vision, O Lord of our hearts. Amen."

- A benediction

    God's blessings are upon us as we finish our work today.

    God's blessings are upon us when we leave here and take up responsibilities at home.

    God's blessings are upon us when we remember the great family of which we are a part and from where we came.

    God's blessings are upon us when we open ourselves to say yes to what lies ahead without knowing that future fully.

    God's blessings are upon us when we find ourselves unable to say yes.

    God's blessings are upon you.

    God's blessings are upon me.

    God's blessings are

    God's blessings.

    Amen.

Adapted from "Words of Worship," William C. Kerley. Originally printed in *The American Baptist*, March 1980. Used by permission.

Be Thou My Vision

Irish, 8th Century

Traditional Irish melody

1. Be thou my vision, O Lord of my heart;
2. Be thou my wisdom, and thou my true word;
3. Riches I heed not, nor man's empty praise,
4. High King of heaven, my victory won.

Naught be all else to me, save that thou art
I ever with thee and save thou with me, Lord;
Thou mine inheritance, now and always:
May I reach heaven's joys, O bright heavn's Sun!

Thou my best thought, by day or by night,
Thou my great Father, I thy true son;
Thou and thou only, first in my heart,
Heart of my own heart, whatever befall,

Waking or sleeping, thy presence my light.
Thou in me dwelling, and I with thee one.
High King of heaven, my treasure thou art.
Still be my vision, O Ruler of all.

This hymn is in public domain and may be reproduced for use in your congregation.

Embracing the Future: A Guide for Reshaping Your Church's Teaching Ministry

Learning...
for Shaping a Vision

Enter into study
    with a view to the future,
    while learning from the past and present.

Remember the words from the Gospel of Mark (4:9): "Let anyone with ears to hear listen!" (NRSV)

Invite others to join you in study as fits your situation and as people express interest.

Use any of the following study resources or techniques or those from your own rich storehouse.

From the Bible

Read and discuss any or all of the following Scripture passages:
    Isaiah 43:14-21

What is the nature of the new thing God is about to do?
    Ezekiel 36:26-28

What might be some of the characteristics of the new heart and/or new spirit God gives?
    Habakkuk 2:1-3

What do we learn about the meaning and power of vision from the writer of Habakkuk?
    Revelation 21:1-5

What is the nature of the new things God is already doing?

From leaders in the field of Christian education

Choose one of the following books as a study book for your group. See this chapter's **RESOURCES** for details.

Charting Our Course: Renewing the Church's Teaching Ministry, Linda R. Isham.

Educating Congregations: The Future of Christian Education, Charles R. Foster.

Mapping Christian Education: Approaches to Congregational Learning, Jack L. Seymour, editor.

Soul Stories: African American Christian Education, Anne Streaty Wimberly.

From the larger world

Read the following. See this chapter's *RESOURCES* for details.

The Fifth Discipline, Peter M. Senge.

From others

1. Call neighboring churches and find out who has vision statements. Ask them to send a copy to you and find out who might talk with you about the process used.

2. Call your region or judicatory office to get names and phone numbers of churches with vision statements. Contact those for more information.

3. Check the Internet for possible information sources on shaping vision statements.

4. Keep your eyes and ears open for vision statements. Keep an awareness of shaping a vision on your back burner as you watch TV, listen to the radio, read the newspaper, go shopping, eat out, are in conversation with others. You might become aware of corporate vision statements as you go about your daily routine. Share and critique them with the planning group.

Sharing...
for Shaping a Vision

Be prepared to share with the larger congregation
   your vision statement,
and to invite them to participate in shaping a vision,
or in responding to a draft of the vision.

•

Remember the words of Teilhard de Chardin: "The
greatest force for the advancement of the human
species is a great hope held in common."

Use any or all of the following ways to involve and
communicate with the congregation as you shape a
vision for your church's teaching ministry.

1. Invite interested individuals to join you in the
    process outlined in this chapter.

2. Invite people to respond to these two incomplete
    sentences:

    "What first interested me and/or continues to
    excite me about the teaching ministry of this
    church is. . . ."

    "What disappoints me about the teaching
    ministry of this church is. . . ."

One way to do this is to have a "graffiti wall" (a place
for people to write their ideas and interact with others) on a bulletin board. Invite people—children,
youth, and adults—to write their responses there.

3. Ask for feedback on the five (or whatever num-
    ber you decided on) components of a vision
    statement. List them in your church newsletter
    and ask for responses.

4. Develop a litany around the components of your
    vision statement and include it in a service of
    worship.

5. Share your draft of a vision statement with the
    congregation—in as many and appropriate ways
    as possible—church newsletter, web site, wor-
    ship bulletin, bulletin board, minutes of your
    group, in person with boards or committees of
    the church.

6. Share your draft of a vision statement with other
    church committees and with the church govern-
    ing body so that it may be looked at in relation to
    other vision statements and the church's overall
    vision statement, if there is one. And if no such
    other vision statements exist, then perhaps your
    work will encourage dialog with other groups
    and/or encourage them to do similar work.

7. Get the statement approved by the appropriate
    church body so it has a larger sanction than just
    your small group.

8. Eventually, when finalized and approved by the
    appropriate bodies of your church, use it as part
    of a Christian education brochure. Have some-
    one develop a logo from it or have someone
    incorporate it into a banner or poster. Use it
    when you announce programs and ministries.
    Post it in classrooms and where study groups
    meet.

Resources...
for Shaping a Vision

Christian Education

Foster, Charles R., *Educating Congregations: The Future of Christian Education,* (Nashville: Abingdon Press, 1994). A look at what is wrong and suggestions on how to fix it that address making meaning, building community, and nurturing hope.

Harris, Maria, and Gabriel Moran *Reshaping Religious Education: Conversations on Contemporary Practice,* (Louisville: Westminster John Knox, 1998). Written conversationally, this book addresses such foundational issues as curriculum, aims, and teaching plus development and spirituality.

Isham, Linda R., *Charting Our Course: Renewing the Church's Teaching Ministry,* (Valley Forge, PA: Judson Press, 1997). Observations about what is needed in the present time to chart a course for the church's teaching ministry in a new century. Filled with practical ideas and helps as well.

Seymour, Jack L., editor, *Mapping Christian Education: Approaches to Congregational Learning,* (Nashville: Abingdon Press, 1997). Exploration of four themes: transformation, faith community, spiritual growth, and religious instruction.

Wimberly, Anne Streaty, *Soul Stories: African American Christian Education,* (Nashville: Abingdon Press, 1994). Describes a story-linking process and invites teachers and leaders to engage in the process and guide others in it.

Vision and Leadership in the Church and World

Barna, George, *The Power of Vision: How You Can Capture and Apply God's Vision for Your Ministry,* (Ventura, CA: Regal Books, 1992). Offers a perspective on vision especially for clergy.

Friend, Howard E. Jr., *Recovering the Sacred Center: Church Renewal from the Inside Out,* (Valley Forge, PA: Judson Press, 1998). The author suggests that the place to begin in renewing the church is by churches and individuals looking inward. A reflective approach is described.

Morris, Danny E., and Charles M. Olsen, *Discerning God's Will Together: A Spiritual Practice for the Church,* (Nashville: The Upper Room, 1997). Shows discernment as an interactive means of making decisions and loving one another in the process.

Rinehart, Stacy T., *Upside Down: The Paradox of Servant Leadership,* (Colorado Springs: NavPress, 1998). The author writes about servant leadership as the kind of leadership Jesus practiced. •

Senge, Peter M., *The Fifth Discipline: The Art and Practice of the Learning Organization,* (New York: Currency Doubleday, 1994). Offers an organic approach consistent with the understanding of the church as the body of Christ.

Comment Sheet

We are eager to learn from users what has been helpful, has worked or not, or could have worked better, as well as what you have been able to accomplish with the help of this resource. Please take a few minutes to respond to the following questions and then send them to the address listed below. Use additional pages as needed.

1. These comments are in response to the following steps/chapters [please check the appropriate step(s) or chapter(s)]:
    ___ Seeing the Big Picture and Getting Started
    ___ Picturing the Future
    ___ Stating Our Mission
    ___ Assessing Our Situation
    ___ Shaping a Vision
    ___ Celebrating and Letting Go
    ___ Developing a Menu of Possibilities
    ___ Making an Action Plan

2. The most helpful part of this step in the planning process was . . .

3. The least helpful part of this step in the planning process was . . .

4. Changes you should consider are . . .

5. Consider adding the following resource(s) to the resource list:

6. Our key accomplishments related to this step of the planning process are . . .

7. Additional comments:

Thanks! Please return your comments to: Marcia Jessen, Educational Ministries, ABC/USA, P.O. Box 851, Valley Forge, PA 19482-0851; 610-768-2056 FAX; marcia.jessen@abc-usa.org

CHAPTER 6

Celebrating and Letting Go

by Dennis Plourde

by Dennis Plourde

PURPOSE:

✔ celebrate and honor the past of our Christian education through a variety of activities such as worship, storytelling, and songs

✔ let go of some parts of the past and allow God to build upon that past for a new future

---

"If we don't hold the annual picnic, people will complain. And I'll be one of them," grumbled Kate. "Even if lately nobody has come and, as you say, it takes a lot of time and energy that could be used elsewhere, you can't just dump something so special from our yearly program."

"I was thinking," Stu offered, "what if we did it up really big this year as a final picnic? We could make a special effort to get a lot of people there, celebrate the history in worship that morning, present awards and recognize those who've always been a part of it. That way it will be more like saying good-bye to an old friend than 'dumping it.'"

Hear the words of the prophet Isaiah: "Do not remember the former things, or consider the things of old. I am about to do a new thing; now it springs forth, do you not perceive it? I will make a way in the wilderness and rivers in the desert" (Isaiah 43:18-19, NRSV). Geoffry W. Grogan, commenting in *The Expositor's Bible Commentary* on these verses, explains that the prophet did not mean for us to ignore the past, but that the past must not stereotype our image of God.

We are meant to reflect on the past with gratitude and stimulated faith but not to allow it to stereotype our expectations from God. Here God affirms—in detail and with emphasis on the deadly efficiency of his deeds. . . . He had made a way through the waters; now he would make a new way—through the desert![1]

Lesslie Newbigin, in *Proper Confidence,* writes: "The church was the bearer of the story. The story shaped the church. As a continued lived narrative, of which contemporary life was a part, the narrative gave shape to public life."[2] Kennon L. Callahan puts it another way: "God has ordained the mission, not the structures."[3] However, in many of our churches we often are confronted with people who believe that the structure was also ordained by God.

The purpose of this chapter is to help us honor, celebrate, and grieve the structures of the past by remembering, honoring, and celebrating the people, events, and images of yesterday that have helped frame our today. We want to thank God for the power of their ministry in our midst and the impact that they have had on both the life of the church and on us personally. After we have identified and celebrated the past, we need to move ahead to the mission of tomorrow assured of the promise that God is able to bring new experiences, events, adventures, and opportunities our way in which we again discover new ways through the wilderness and renew the church for Christian education ministry tomorrow.

Illustration #1: A Packet of Seeds

I write this on a cold, damp summer's day in Scotland. It is not supposed to be this cold, and even the hearty Scots are grumbling. Gardens are not growing, holidays are being dampened by the cold, and life is miserable. In front of my writing table is a packet of Sutton seeds, Limnanthes *(douglasii)*, the "Poached Egg Plant." They are resting comfortably in the "special" foil package, sealed with this warning: "Seed in enclosed sealed packet is dried to preserve high germination. Once opened the packet should not be resealed as seed will have absorbed atmospheric moisture and normal aging will have begun." In other words, these seeds have a life, and at this point they should be at the perfect condition for planting—once opened they begin a process that will eventually lead to death—aging. I am presented with at least three options: (1) leave them sealed in their package, sterile, useless, but at the right stage of perfection; (2) open and let the atmospheric moisture begin the aging and dying process; or (3) the preferred option, open, plant, and nurture them so that they may obtain their highest potential. Even in this process they will die, but in dying they will find life, and in a few short weeks the border of the garden will be laden with "many yellow flowers with white edges on lovely feathery foliage. Attractive to bees!"

The promise of a beautiful border surrounding the garden will only happen if the seeds are allowed to die. Then their beauty will be enjoyed, eyes will delight in the delicate color of the blossoms, and bees will be able to frolic from flower to flower getting the necessary nectar for future honey. The seeds must die to give way to the power and potential that is within them. Once they are planted, nurtured, gently and lovingly cared for, weeded, and watered, they will burst forth in a magnificent display of beauty far different from the tiny seeds planted in the spring earth. However, as long as they are kept where they are, sealed in a packet on the window sill in a tightly controlled environment, nothing will happen. The potential for new life and beauty will remain only potential. Only when they are set free, when they are allowed to die, will they surrender themselves to the potential that God has created in them. In dying there is life. In surrender there is resurrection. Pushing through the soil will not be a seed, but a new life, a new form, a new being, green and lush filling the garden with color and beauty—a new form, a new creation. Risk must be taken to let the seeds go and develop into a new creation.

Collage of Yesterday

Materials Needed: pictures of the past, 3" x 5" cards, pens/pencils, scissors, tape or glue, a large poster board or display area, and creativity

- Gather pictures of past church members, events, and programs. You may want to have some of these reproduced if you want to keep them for future reference.

- Identify as many people, events, and dates as possible. It may be helpful to number each segment and have someone write a narrative for each picture.

- Make a collage of the past—it could be in the form of a cross, a ship, or whatever creative pattern you come up with.

- Display it for several weeks in an appropriate, well-traveled place where people can see, remember, and talk about the past.

- Plan a worship service celebrating the past. Honor teachers, youth leaders, and others who have given years of service to make the past possible. Print mini biographies of these individuals and events. Thank those present who had a part. If there are members who have moved away, are in nursing homes, and so forth, compose letters to be sent to them thanking them for their contributions. Give the Collage of Yesterday a place of prominence in the worship space.

  Prelude (use old choruses such as The *B-I-B-L-E, This Little Light of Mine, Stop and Let Me Tell You, Everybody Ought to Know*)

  Call to Worship (write one that celebrates the past)

  Hymn (use an old favorite)

  Invocation

  Chorus time (sing old Sunday school/youth songs)

  Prayer (invite those present to offer prayers of thanksgiving for teachers and Christian education leaders and events of the past, asking God's blessing on the present as well)

  Offering (remind worshipers of the "living sacrifices" that have been given and give 3" x 5" cards to everyone and invite them to write the names of people who have been "living sacrifices" on behalf of this congregation's teaching ministry, people important in their own growth in faith)

  Sermon (if you dare, invite members of the congregation to share and celebrate the past of this church's teaching ministry, then let your contribution be toward the future—the making of new memories, new collages, for the next generation)

  Hymn (choose a contemporary one and let the emphasis turn to moving to a new day, time, and vision for the future)

  Benediction (use words that move the community from reflecting on the past to present and future challenges before the people of God)

This packet of seeds could also be used to describe where Christian education is as we end one millennium and plunge into another. We have packets of seed, filled with potential, waiting to be planted and allowed to unleash the dawning of a new creation. The old forms have now produced the new seed, and we have in our hands the seeds of tomorrow. Unfortunately, we do not have a pretty picture on the outside of the package telling us what the new product, once mature, will look like. We do not know its beauty or its fragrance. Our faith must be in the One who provided us with the seeds, who challenges us to plant them, and who will nurture them into new life and hope for the church. God waits for us to take a step of faith and allow the seeds "to fall to the ground and die." It is never easy to give up our traditions of tried and proven methods, our ways of doing things, and allow the fresh creative breeze of the Holy Spirit to blow through and produce new and exciting life, a life of fragrance and beauty with potential to color the world.

The question is, will we plant the seeds? Will we water them, nourish them, and give them the opportunity to grow and bloom in the garden of Christian education? We may not know what the beauty of their flowers will be, but neither did those who planted the seeds before know how we would bloom. We need to give the new seeds an opportunity to engage in new and different styles of Christian education that will equip the saints (present and future) for the challenges of tomorrow.

Illustration #2: Music Before the Instruments

Harry Emerson Fosdick, in *The Secret of Victorious Living,*[4] observed that Beethoven's music is best played on instruments that had not been invented when Beethoven was alive. The orchestra in Beethoven's day would not have included the piccolo, bass clarinets, double bassoons, trombones, tubas, percussion instruments, or harps. The wind instruments of his day would not have the range of the stringed instruments because the technology had not as yet been introduced that would give the wind instruments the level of range that they now enjoy. Beethoven's music is enjoyed more today because of the instruments that it is now played on, than when it was first introduced. Imagine how poor our appreciation of his work would be if music purists insisted that his music could be played only on the instruments for which it was written.

Isn't this what we often do in the church in Christian education? We insist that the music can only be played on the instruments that were around when the music was written. Imagine owning a keyboard with a wide range of instrumentation and not ever trying an instrument other than the piano. We would be wasting a valuable instrument and we would also be limiting our own experiences. The task for the church today is to allow the seeds to be planted and the music to be played.

Congregational Psalm

(an interactive worship service that includes composing a psalm as part of the experience)

Materials Needed: sheets of paper or 4" x 6" cards, pens/pencils, modern translations of the Psalms (printed in poetry form)

Prelude

Call to worship (a reading of one of the historical psalms—not the whole psalm but enough to give the flavor of a historical psalm that celebrates the past and God's guiding hand)

Hymn

Invocation

Readings (more psalms—antiphonal, responsive—varying how they are presented)

Composing a psalm

Divide congregation into groups of five or six persons—young and old. Select group leaders in advance.

Have paper and pens or pencils available and ask each group to write five or six lines of a psalm to celebrate your church's Christian education history.

Play quiet, worshipful music in the background.

Allow 10 minutes.

Sharing psalms with the congregation

Hymn (one that celebrates God's work in history)

Message (Build on the psalms just shared. Express thanks to God for the witness and witnesses of the past. Raise the question about the stories that will be told by the next generation of your congregation. Challenge those present to continue to let God move in your midst)

Hymn

Benediction

Moving Beyond Yesterday

The most difficult path facing us is not in honoring or celebrating the past but in moving away from the past into a new, exciting, challenging, and sometimes frightening tomorrow (we all have fear of the unknown, do not like to wander in the wilderness unsure of our destination, or step out into the unknown). This chapter includes suggestions to help you and your congregation honor both past events and the people who made them possible and to give some form of closure to those ministries that no longer convey living truths. There is no intent to suggest that every ministry or program from the past needs to be ended. This is a time for reflecting on those things that may have become dying customs rather than living truths. Once closure is achieved, it is then possible to develop a menu of possibilities for the future (see chapter 7). The **PRAYING, LEARNING,** and **SHARING** pages in this chapter offer suggestions to help you in preparing to celebrate and let go of those teaching ministries or programs that have served you faithfully in the past but now need to be set aside and to look forward with hope to new and faithful teaching ministries in the future.

In shaded boxes found throughout this chapter, you will find ways to honor and celebrate the past. They are intended to help a congregation or small group honor and celebrate the ministry of both people and programs in the ministry of the past. They are designed to help bring closure to a past ministry; and when closure has been achieved, movement can be made into the wonderful opportunities awaiting the body of Christ in the coming days of a new century. Each design is only a suggestion. Use any or all of them and adapt them to your situation. Additional ideas may be found in the resources listed in this chapter's **RESOURCES**. Share with us how you have used these so that in future revisions of this material your stories may also be told.

But first a word about closure. When the following true story was told to me, my first thought was "How ridiculous." But after reflecting on the experience, it makes more and more sense—because it provided needed closure.

The women's society had been a part of First Church for as long as anyone could remember. It faithfully had raised money for the church and for missions and had assisted in keeping the church going in lean years. Now its members were aging and dying and new members were not being attracted to the group. Realistically it had only a few more years of life. The remaining members decided that because of their ages and inability to do much the group should disband. However, there was much discussion as to what to do with the gavel that had been used to open and close the meetings since their inception. The pastor was approached to conduct a service, and the gavel was buried in an appropriate place in the church garden. This simple act honored these women and their past, allowed them to grieve their loss, and gave closure to their ministry. It also gave the congregation a chance to recognize their contributions and to grieve with them. Once the gavel was buried, they were free to move on.

What happens after we have experienced closure? If we fail to fill in the void that has been, then the old "demons" may return with even more determination to keep things just as they were. Or we may have a void that will never be filled. This resource has been designed to help you evaluate where you are, recognize those pieces from the past that may need to be celebrated, honored, and moved beyond, and to discover ways in which new ministries can be developed. It is an envisioning tool to help open the church to vital, changing, refreshing winds of the Spirit of God. Do not stop here. Move on and discover the enriching possibilities that await those who "walk by faith."

Footprints

(an activity that can be used in a Sunday church school or all-church event or informal worship, involving all ages)

Materials Needed: construction paper (several colors), pencils or pens, scissors
Time Needed: 45–60 minutes

- Trace the footprints of everyone present on construction paper (shoes may be left on). Pair people up to do this. People may wish to put their names on their footprints.

- Cut out the footprints.

- Place the footprints (in a path) around the room or sanctuary. Be intentional on how they are placed. Begin by placing adult footprints. As the path grows, add some of the youth and children's footprints on top of the adult ones. Then as the path comes to an end, have only the children's foot prints.

- Discuss why only adult footprints appear at the beginning. If needed, indicate that they represent the generation that has been a part of the congregation in past years. The children's and youth footprints on top of the adult footprints represent the new generation coming along, learning from the older generation. But note, the older ones stop and the new generation takes over—each generation must leave its own footprints on the sands of time. The footprints are symbolic of letting go and letting a new generation move forward into tomorrow.

Notes

1. Frank E. Gaebelein, ed., *The Expositor's Bible Commentary*, vol. 6 (Grand Rapids: Zondervan, 1986), 261.

2. Lesslie Newbigin, *Proper Confidence* (Grand Rapids, MI: Eerdman's, 1995), 53.

3. Kennon L. Callahan, *Effective Church Leadership: Building on the Twelve Keys* (San Francisco: HarperSanFrancisco, 1990), 203.

4. Harry Emerson Fosdick, *The Secret of Victorious Living* (New York: Harper & Bros., 1934), 95-96.

Praying...

for Celebrating and Letting Go

Enter into prayer with grateful hearts.

Then let us, with the Spirit's
    daring,
step from the past,
    and leave behind
our disappointment, guilt
    and grieving,
seeking new paths,
    and sure to find.

Taken from *This Is a Day of New Beginnings* by Brian Wren ©
1983, 1987 Hope Publishing Co., Carol Stream, IL 60188. All
rights reserved. Used by permission.

Use the following prayers as you prepare to celebrate your church's teaching ministry and to anticipate letting go of those ministries and programs that
no longer serve you well.

God of all grace,
You are larger
than the grasp
of our hands
or head.
When we want
to hold on to
things
just as they are,
give us the trust
to let go
of them
in order that
they might become
what they can be.
Amen.

By George Graham. From *Alive Now,* May/June 1998. Copyright
by the Upper Room. Used by permission.

Gathered in the Spirit

Jesus said good-bye to friends,
    and left this earth,
but did not abandon those
    who did not understand.

The Holy Spirit came
    to comfort, to guide,
    to bring peace—
to teach people to sing
    through their sorrow,
    and to live.

And in life's changes
    as [we] release,
    relinquish
well-loved people and places
    to God in prayer,
[We] sense that these are not lost to [us],
    but are gathered by the Spirit,
    brought together in the process
to comfort, to guide, to bring peace,
    to help [us] sing
    through the sorrow,
    and to live.

Adapted from Roberta Porter, "Gathered in the Spirit," (*Alive Now,*
May/June 1998, 27.) Used by permission.

Learning...
for Celebrating and Letting Go

As you prepare to involve the larger church family in celebrating and letting go of your past Christian education, plan to continue to grow in your own understanding of that past and the importance of celebrating and letting go of the pieces that no longer serve the congregation well.

Ways to do that include:

1. Do together as a planning team the activities you are planning for the congregation.

2. Explore the meaning of "remembering," "celebrating," "thanksgiving," "grieving," and "letting go."

3. Study Scriptures such as Deuteronomy 6:20-25; Isaiah 43:18-19; Luke 22:14-20.

4. Reflect on the meaning of these words of Marjorie J. Thompson:

   > "Many in the church today view Christian tradition as impeding creative change. But the irony is that the truest aspects of Christian tradition are the most radically creative and life-changing. Indeed, tradition itself provides us with criteria for 'sorting living truths from dying customs.'" (*Soul Feast* [Louisville: Westminster John Knox, 1995], 13)

Sharing...
for Celebrating and Letting Go

SHARING

As your planning team anticipates celebrations in the life of the congregation, be regular and faithful in communicating your plans. You may find some of the following suggestions helpful.

1. From the start gain the support of the pastor and governing body of your church.

2. Ask to visit with the governing body, tell them the ideas you are working on, and guide them in a simple exercise of giving thanks and letting go—briefly listing those parts of your church's past ministries for which they are most grateful and those that they most miss. Talk about the importance of remembering, but not clinging to, the past and of letting go of those events, programs, and ministries that have become dying customs. Ask for their support of the events you are planning.

3. Ask someone from the governing body to join your planning team.

4. Promote widely the events and activities you are planning and allow plenty of time to get them on the church calendar. Find unusual ways, places, and times to drop hints of what is to come.

5. If you plan to do a collage of yesterday, involve as many people as possible in gathering photos and archival items and in identifying people and events.

6. If your church has a history committee or church historian, involve that person in your planning.

7. Interview older members of the church to gain insights about the past.

8. Use one of the church bulletin boards to build a Christian education time line for your church. Invite people to add events and to indicate when they first got involved. Leave it up for a period of time.

Resources...

for Celebrating and Letting Go

"Farewells," the May/June 1998 issue of *Alive Now,* a bimonthly publication of the Upper Room, Nashville, 1-800-972-0433. Contains poems, essays, prayers, and Scripture.

Friend, Howard E. Jr., *Recovering the Sacred Center: Church Renewal from the Inside Out,* (Valley Forge, PA: Judson Press, 1998). The author's process for renewal offers helpful insights for looking at the past and what hinders those who have a mind toward the future.

Isham, Linda R., *Charting Our Course: Renewing the Church's Teaching Ministry,* (Valley Forge, PA: Judson Press, 1997). Chapter 1 has a brief section on grieving and release.

Morgan, Richard L., *Remembering Your Story: A Guide to Spiritual Autobiography,* (Nashville: Upper Room Books, 1996). While focused on storytelling for older adults, there are insights here for the church as it remembers, celebrates, and lets go.

Spritzer, Lee B., *Endless Possibilities: Exploring the Journeys of Your Life,* (Lincoln, NE: Spiritual Journey Press, 1997). A book and workbook for helping individuals and congregations share spiritual journeys.

RESOURCES

Comment Sheet

We are eager to learn from users what has been helpful, has worked or not, or could have worked better, as well as what you have been able to accomplish with the help of this resource. Please take a few minutes to respond to the following questions and then send them to the address listed below. Use additional pages as needed.

1. These comments are in response to the following steps/chapters [please check the appropriate step(s) or chapter(s)]:
    ___ Seeing the Big Picture and Getting Started
    ___ Picturing the Future
    ___ Stating Our Mission
    ___ Assessing Our Situation
    ___ Shaping a Vision
    ___ Celebrating and Letting Go
    ___ Developing a Menu of Possibilities
    ___ Making an Action Plan

2. The most helpful part of this step in the planning process was . . .

3. The least helpful part of this step in the planning process was . . .

4. Changes you should consider are . . .

5. Consider adding the following resource(s) to the resource list:

6. Our key accomplishments related to this step of the planning process are . . .

7. Additional comments:

Thanks! Please return your comments to: Marcia Jessen, Educational Ministries, ABC/USA, P.O. Box 851, Valley Forge, PA 19482-0851; 610-768-2056 FAX; marcia.jessen@abc-usa.org

CHAPTER 7

Developing a Menu of Possibilities

by Linda R. Isham

"Now we're ready to list a whole host of ideas and suggestions for our teaching ministry. Let's put the creativity permission meter at 10! Later we can pull in the reins," Imogene remarked, noticing a room full of nodding heads. "Just remember, we want the ideas to reflect the mission and vision for this church's teaching ministry."

T his step is one for idea people. The tasks may seem less theoretical and more practical, and that sense of concreteness is appealing to many of us and makes us feel closer to implementation. Through the course of this step you will be developing a broad list (menu) of possible teaching ministries, programs, and/or actions for your church. The next step (making an action plan) will have you narrowing down the list of many good and wonderful possibilities to the ones best suited for your situation at this given time. It might be helpful to point out that there is a fine line between when this step ends and the step of making an action plan begins. There are no rules saying you can't step over the line!

If you have already completed all steps except "making an action plan," then you have a lot of information and ideas to build on as you develop a menu of possible teaching/learning actions, ministries, or programs for your church. This step can be seen as a logical outgrowth from assessing your situation and shaping a vision. Indeed, you may already have noted possibilities as you have worked on other steps. If so, I hope you can retrieve them now. If, however, you are starting the process with this step, you will be beginning from scratch and at some point will benefit by completing the other steps in the process. They will serve to validate, or

not, the options in your menu. Or you may just want to focus on developing a menu of better possibilities for your teaching ministry.

Organizational Approaches

Before outlining the tasks within this step of the planning process, let's think for a moment about organizational approaches to the actions, programs, or ministries that make up a church's teaching ministry menu. Most churches currently use an organizational approach we might call programmatic. We have programs such as the Sunday church school, vacation Bible school, and youth groups, and our planning is done around those programs with perhaps a Christmas program, Easter program, and Children's Day program added.

There are some other organizational approaches we might consider. While they may end up with programs, they don't start there. They assume that the teaching ministry belongs to the whole church and not just to teachers or a group assigned responsibility for Christian education. That's good news for all of us—the church, teachers, and the group assigned responsibility for Christian education in the congregation. It means that we are partners in an important ministry of the church. None of us works in isolation, and teaching is seen as integrally related to ministries of worship, service, and fellowship.

Maria Harris, in her book *Fashion Me a People: Curriculum in the Church,* says that curriculum is the entire course of the church's life. Then she goes on to spell out the curriculum of teaching, fellowship, worship, proclamation, and service.[1] Her conceptual framework can be helpful to us as we think about organizational approaches to the church's teaching ministry.

In the 1970s Rachel Henderlite reminded us that community life was the principal educator for a congregation. "In my judgment, the only way in which such faith as this can be elicited is through inclusion in a community of faith where the whole life of the community is shaped and governed by the community's commitment to the Lord."[2] She believed that congregational life is a key curriculum in the education of its members, and if there is a disparity between what we say and what we do, what we do is more likely to be internalized.[3]

So let's think about some organizational approaches. One such approach is ordered around the faith life cycle and its teachable moments. Such teachable moments occur at baptism or dedication, presenting Bibles to children, profession of faith, confirmation or baptism, Communion/Lord's Supper, graduation, marriage, birth of children, vocational choices, retirement, and death. Most of these moments have worship, fellowship, and teaching possibilities within them.

Another approach is organized around the church year—Advent, Christmas, Epiphany, Lent, Easter, Pentecost, and ordinary times. We might add to the church year observances from our denominational or community calendar including World Communion Sunday, National Observance of Children's Sabbath, Reformation Sunday, Stewardship Sunday, Thanksgiving, Martin Luther King Day, Christian Unity Sunday, World Day of Prayer, Peace Sunday, Family Week, Religious Liberty Sunday, Children's Day, as well as denominational offerings. Again most of these have worship, fellowship, and teaching possibilities inherent in them.

Charles R. Foster speaks about "event-full" education, suggesting that a church order its teaching ministry around events that form and transform individuals and the community. In his book *Educating Congregations: The Future of Christian Education,* he describes four kinds of formative events: paradigmatic events, seasonal events, occasional events, and unexpected events. He goes on to write, "The education of the community around the events that give structure and momentum to its life involves three movements: . . . **preparation . . . engagement . . . mutually critical reflection.**"[4]

Within any approach we choose to take we need to think about teaching occurring in one-on-one mentoring or apprenticeship relationships, in small groups, and with the total congregation. Providing for both age-specific groupings and intergenerational groupings is important. We need to be aware that teaching often occurs unintentionally by example, sometimes by design in intentional groups and classes, and by the community's tradition. And we'll want to think about what is best taught by example, by design, and by tradition; or best taught in a classroom, on a mission project or trip, in morning worship, or when the community of faith is gathered for fellowship.

We'll want to think about what we want to teach and learn and when is the best time. For example, when and how is the best time to teach and learn Bible stories, Bible study skills, biblical interpretation, church history, denominational mission and ministries, leadership skills, spiritual disciplines, how to pray and worship, and how to serve and do acts of justice, and so forth.

Other organizational approaches may come to your mind. Consider what will work best for you and be prepared to list possibilities with that approach in mind and to experiment within such a framework. Finding an organizational approach for our teaching ministry menu of possibilities is a task in the preparation movement of which Foster speaks.

Things to Keep in Mind

As we approach this step of developing a menu of possible teaching/learning actions, ministries, and programs, there are a couple of things we need to keep in mind: (1) our mission and vision, and (2) our organizational approach. Let's review each of these.

Keeping Mission and Vision at the Forefront

It is important not to lose sight of your mission and vision as you journey ahead in this planning process. Once you have some possible teaching/learning actions, programs, and/or ministries, take a look at them in light of your mission and vision.

Determining an Organizational Approach

It is helpful to reflect first on your community's life, tradition, and mission and then consider how they inform the way you will organize for Christian education. You may find that some of the organizational approaches outlined earlier in this chapter would suit your situation, or you may determine other ways. If nothing else, take time to think more deeply about organizing for teaching before or as you decide on programs you will have during the course of a year. Your mission and vision statements might also point you in the direction of an organizational approach.

You will find suggestions to guide you in determining an organizational approach(es) in the box headed Organizational Approach.

Organizational Approach

Materials Needed: newsprint, felt-tip markers, and masking tape
Time Needed: 45–60 minutes each

There are several ways you might begin thinking about an organizational approach. Three are described here. Choose one of these or one of your own.

A. Key events observed by your congregation.

1. List key events observed by your congregation. A sample list from one church includes Homecoming Sunday, Christian Education Sunday, World Communion Sunday, All Saints Day, Stewardship Sunday, Thanksgiving, Advent Workshop, Community Advent Walk, caroling, Christmas Eve service, Epiphany, Martin Luther King Day observance, hymn sing with a sister church, Lenten breakfasts, monthly soup kitchen, clothing closet, Covenant to Care, Maundy Thursday service with sister church, community Good Friday service, Palm Sunday baptisms, Easter, Youth Sunday, Laity Sunday, monthly men's breakfast, weekday preschool, weekly circle of prayer, youth groups, Sunday church school, Peace Sunday, Children's Day, summer worship at historic church, strawberry supper, turkey supper, church-wide thanksgiving dinner.

2. Divide the list among the group and, working in pairs, note how individuals and the congregation are or could be educated by the events assigned to them.

3. Come together to share these and offer them to the group.

B. Five forms of ministry.

1. Assign the following five forms of ministry to five different individuals or small groups: teaching, fellowship, worship, proclamation, and service.

2. Ask each group or individual to list on a sheet of newsprint five ways the congregation or individuals are educated by this form. Use your lists as you begin developing your list of possible teaching/learning actions, programs, and ministries.

C. Church year events.

1. List church year events (such as Advent, Christmas, Lent, and so forth) that your church observes.

2. In small groups, or working as one group, list ways the congregation and individuals are taught in/by each of these.

Sample List of Possibilities

A sample list of possibilities, growing out of the Old New Century Church vision statement (see chapter 5), might be helpful to consider before you begin your own work.

VISION COMPONENT: *Walk with those we call to lead and teach others.*

MENU OF POSSIBILITIES:

50 percent of the church membership completing a gifts identification and affirmation process this year

placing apprentice teachers in at least half of our church school classes or Bible study groups during the fall quarter

having ten potential small-group leaders complete a training course by January 1

assigning prayer partners for every teacher and leader in our church's teaching ministry this year

developing a resource center with the latest videos, CDs, audiotapes, books, and periodicals

assigning mentors to new teachers

Getting Ready

The purpose of this step is to develop as broad and long a list as possible of teaching ministries programs, and actions. One way to do this is by brainstorming (see Reproducible Sheet 9). In brainstorming everyone's idea is recorded and there is no discussion about the merits of the ideas. The intent is to gather a large number of ideas as quickly as possible and to give everyone the opportunity to speak if they wish. It assumes that discussion, analysis, and prioritizing—even objectives—will follow.

In preparation for your work on this step, decide how you will involve the larger congregation. If you have completed other steps in this planning process, have the appropriate data from those available as you develop a menu of possibilities. Set aside enough time to complete this step. The process described will take 1½–2 hours to complete. It may be beneficial to spend time in prayer, study, and sharing with others as well. See **PRAYING, LEARNING, SHARING,** and **RESOURCES** in this chapter.

Developing a Menu of Possibilities

Materials Needed: newsprint, felt-tip markers, masking tape, Reproducible Sheet 9
Time Needed: 1½–2 hours

1. Review your mission and vision statements, work done earlier on assessing your situation, and results of your thinking about organizational approach(es). Note any categories that may have surfaced (such as leader development, outreach, teaching/learning models involving the entire congregation). If you have started your planning with this step, work from your organizational approach material.

2. Pause to pray for openness to all ideas and the ability to clearly communicate.

3. Brainstorm (see "Brainstorming Guidelines" Reproducible Sheet 9) strategies under each category you may have decided upon, recording ideas on newsprint. If your group is large, it may be helpful to have two people recording ideas as well as a facilitator.

4. Post the lists for all to see.

5. You may want to gather additional ideas from the larger congregation. You can do this by again using the graffiti wall mentioned in chapter 5, **SHARING.** Provide a framework within which to solicit ideas from children, youth, and adults. Welcome both words and pictures.

   Give people the date by which they will need to add their graffiti. Plan to add ideas gleaned this way with your own brainstorm list(s).

6. Take a break after brainstorming.

7. Determine when you will meet to begin prioritizing and make any assignments that need to be done in the interim.

8. Offer blessings to one another before leaving.

Notes

1. Maria Harris, *Fashion Me a People: Curriculum in the Church* (Louisville: Westminster John Knox, 1989), chapter 3.

2. Rachel Henderlite, "Asking the Right Questions," in *A Colloquy on Christian Education*, John H. Westerhoff III, ed. (Philadelphia: Pilgrim Press, 1972), 204.

3. Carol Lakey Hess and Estelle Rountree McCarthy, "Rachel Henderlite: A Life Lived in Response," in *Faith of Our Foremothers: Women Changing Religious Education*, Barbara Anne Keely, ed. (Louisville: Westminster John Knox, 1997), 64–65.

4. Charles R. Foster, *Educating Congregations: The Future of Christian Education* (Nashville: Abingdon Press, 1994), 47–48.

Praying...

for Developing a Menu of Possibilities

Enter into prayer
    seeking wisdom,
        creativity,
        helpful and clear words,
        ears to hear others' words,
        discernment.
    being open to
        surprises,
        the unexpected,
        not the same old, same old,
        a change in the agenda.

Remember the words of Douglas Steere: "In learning to pray, no laboratory is needed but a room; no apparatus but ourselves. The living God is the field of force into which we enter in prayer, and the only really fatal failure is to stop praying and not to begin again."

Invite the congregation to be in prayer with you, to be prayer partners.

Use any or all of the following prayer resources or those from your own rich storehouse.

- Adapt Ted Loder's prayer to be the prayer of your group.

O God,
who out of nothing
    brought everything that is,
out of what I am
    bring more of what I dream
    but haven't dared;
direct my power and passion
    to creating life
        where there is death,
    to putting flesh of action
        on bare-boned intentions,
    to light fires
        against the midnight of indifference,
    to throwing bridges of care
        across canyons of loneliness;
so I can look on creation,
    together with you,
        and, behold,
            call it very good;
through Jesus Christ my Lord. [Amen][1]

- Listen to these words from Genesis 1:27 and 31:

> "So God created humankind in his image,
> in the image of God he created them; . . .
> God saw everything that he had made,
> and indeed, it was very good." (NRSV)

Reflect on them in silence. Think about what it means to be created in God's image.

Give thanks for your creativity and the creativity of others in the group.

Ask that you might use that creativity without restraint or doubts in the task at hand.

- Sing or read together the words to the hymn "We Travel Toward a Land Unknown"

- A benediction

God's blessings are upon us when our talk and plans become power and creative mission.

God's blessings are upon us when we risk trying something new.

God's blessings are upon us when those efforts hardly seem worth it and when they pay off, so to speak.

God's blessings are upon us each moment.

God's blessings are upon you.

God's blessings are upon me.

God's blessings are

God's blessings.

Amen.

Adapted from William C. Kerley, "Words of Worship." Originally printed in *The American Baptist,* March 1980. Used by permission.

1. Excerpt from *Guerrillas of Grace: Prayers for the Battle* by Ted Loder, copyright 1984. Reprinted by permission of Innisfree Press, Inc. Philadelphia, PA.

We Travel Toward a Land Unknown

Thomas H. Troeger

Carol Doran

1. We trav - el toward a land un - known, God's word our on - ly
2. Then where our free - dom first was won We set - tle down to
3. And when we think the jour - ney's end is ver - y near at
4. We trav - el toward a land un - known, but all a - long the

chart, And breathe in the wind that has swept and blown From that
stay, But find that the jour - ney has just be - gun And the
hand We learn that the road has an - oth - er bend And we're
route We're thank - ing our Lord for the won - ders shown And the

land to the hu - man heart. And on the wind_____ we
wind blows an - oth - er way. And on the wind_____ we
far from the prom - ised land. But then the wind_____ re -
faith that has con - quered doubt. Give thanks the wind_____ is

hear the sound Of Mir - i - am's dance by the sea, And we dance with the slaves whom
hear the song Of Mo - ses and Da - vid and Ruth, Who are giv - ing us strength to
turns and lifts Our heart and our strength and our soul, And we're filled with the stead - fast
blow - ing still, And pray that the church may be blessed With the vis - ion and grace to

Phar - aoh bound But the Lord of hosts set free.
right the wrong And to speak and do the truth.
Christ - like gifts That re - veal a - gain our goal.
do God's will And be faith - ful on its quest.

From *New Hymns for the Life of the Church*
Words: Thomas H. Troeger
Music: Carol Doran
© 1987, Thomas H. Troeger and Carol Doran
Used by permission of Oxford University Press, Inc.

Learning...
for Developing a Menu of Possibilities

Enter into study
    with a view to learning some new ways.

Remember the words of Heinrich Bernd (*A Year in the Maine Woods* [Reading, MA: Addison-Wesley, 1994], 109): "The capacity to wonder allows us to anticipate, and that is a very big adaptive step."

Invite others to join you in study as fits your situation and as people express interest.

Use any of the following:

- Assign people to read up on and/or research and report on topics such as those listed below or ones you have identified as important for your situation:

    volunteerism in today's world

    computer-assisted teaching/learning

    the Christian year

    "event-centered" education in the church

    curriculum as the entire course of the church's life

    ministry with children

    ministry with youth

    ministry with young adults

    ministry with middle adults

    ministry with older adults

    spiritual formation

    small groups

    gifts identification and affirmation

    inviting, encouraging, and equipping teachers and leaders

    new models

    resource centers

    theological questions

- Talk with others (in neighboring churches, in your denomination, in your community, newcomers in your church) about what they are doing by way of teaching ministries, programs, and activities.

- Keep questions such as the following in mind as you talk with others:

    What are the most exciting things you are doing?

    Who is giving leadership?

    How did the programs/ministries get started?

    How are people responding?

    What are the pitfalls others should avoid?

    What are the keys to your programs/ ministries' success?

    What have you learned while doing these programs/ministries?

- Check the web sites of your national or regional denominational offices and of other churches in your denomination for creative programming ideas in the area of Christian education.

LEARNING

Sharing...

for Developing a Menu of Possibilities

Be prepared to involve others in developing the menu and to communicate what you're about.

Use any or all of the following ways of involving and/or communicating with the congregation.

1. Invite members of the congregation to share with you innovative programs/ministries in Christian education that they have heard or know about.

2. Invite members to any or all of your planning sessions.

3. Keep the congregation updated on your work through your normal channels—posting your minutes, articles in the church newsletter and/or worship bulletin, items on the web site, in person with key groups in the church, and so forth.

4. Ask for and/or test out ideas on your graffiti wall. With the menu theme in mind, picture a table with a menu on it and ask people to list choices they'd like to see on the menu or have them check the menu items they like best.

Resources...

for Developing a Menu of Possibilities

Blazier, Kenneth D. and Linda R. Isham, editors, *The Teaching Church at Work: A Manual for the Board of Christian Education,* (Valley Forge, PA: Judson Press, 1993). Especially chapters 9, 10, and 11.

Bruce, Barbara, *7 Ways of Teaching the Bible to Children,* (Nashville: Abingdon Press, 1996). Includes twenty-five lessons plus activities that satisfy different learning styles.

Choy-Wong, Kathryn, *Building Bridges: A Handbook for Cross-Cultural Ministry,* (Valley Forge, PA: Judson Press, 1998). Includes suggestions on how to begin, leader training, session outlines, and exercises to use.

Clapp, Steve, and Jerry O. Cook, *Youth Workers Handbook,* (Elgin, IL: FaithQuest, Brethren Press, 1992). The third edition of this book includes current information about young people and their culture, a section on movies and video, and thought-provoking section of the biblical and theological basis of youth work.

Cripe, Douglas D., editor, *Blueprints for Building Christian Education,* (St. Louis: Christian Board of Publication, 1997). Especially chapters 2, 4, 6, 7, and 9.

Crockett, Joseph V., *Teaching Scripture from an African-American Perspective,* (Nashville: Discipleship Resources, 1991). Describes four distinct yet related teaching strategies: story, exile, sanctuary, and exodus.

Foster, Charles R., *Educating Congregations: The Future of Christian Education,* (Nashville: Abingdon Press, 1994). Especially chapter 2.

Halverson, Delia, *32 Ways to Become a Great Sunday School Teacher,* (Nashville: Abingdon Press, 1997). Includes self-directed studies for church school teachers on such things as teaching the Bible creatively, teaching about worship, creating a positive classroom atmosphere, using teachable moments.

Harris, Maria, *Fashion Me a People: Curriculum in the Church,* (Louisville: Westminster John Knox, 1989). Especially chapter 3.

Isham, Linda R., *Charting Our Course: Renewing the Church's Teaching Ministry,* (Valley Forge, PA: Judson Press, 1997). Especially chapters 3, 4, and 5.

Melchert, Charles F., *Wise Teaching: Biblical Wisdom and Educational Ministry,* (Harrisburg, PA: Trinity Press International, 1998). A look at Proverbs, Job, and Ecclesiastes. Note especially the chapter "What Counts as Education in a Wisdom Approach?"

O'Neal, Debbie Trafton, *More Than Glue and Glitter: A Classroom Guide for Volunteer Teachers,* (Minneapolis: Augsburg Fortress, 1992). Filled with practical, creative learning activities and basic teaching techniques.

Osmer, Richard Robert, *Teaching for Faith: A Guide for Teachers of Adult Classes,* (Louisville: Westminster John Knox, 1992). The author explores four dimensions of faith: faith as belief, as commitment, as relationship, and as mystery—and describes teaching approaches that can address each of these dimensions.

Ropp, Steve, *One on One: Making the Most of Your Mentoring Relationship,* (Newton, KS: Faith and Life Press, 1993). Lots of nuts and bolts advice for those who mentor youth. Includes reproducible "share sheets."

Schuller, David S., editor, *Rethinking Christian Education: Explorations in Theory and Practice,* (St. Louis: Chalice Press, 1993). Especially chapters 3, 5–9.

Seymour, Jack L., editor, *Mapping Christian Education: Approaches to Congregational Learning,* (Nashville: Abingdon Press, 1997). Especially chapters 2–5.

RESOURCES

Comment Sheet

We are eager to learn from users what has been helpful, has worked or not, or could have worked better, as well as what you have been able to accomplish with the help of this resource. Please take a few minutes to respond to the following questions and then send them to the address listed below. Use additional pages as needed.

1. These comments are in response to the following steps/chapters [please check the appropriate step(s) or chapter(s)]:

___ Seeing the Big Picture and Getting Started

___ Picturing the Future

___ Stating Our Mission

___ Assessing Our Situation

___ Shaping a Vision

___ Celebrating and Letting Go

___ Developing a Menu of Possibilities

___ Making an Action Plan

2. The most helpful part of this step in the planning process was . . .

3. The least helpful part of this step in the planning process was . . .

4. Changes you should consider are . . .

5. Consider adding the following resource(s) to the resource list:

6. Our key accomplishments related to this step of the planning process are . . .

7. Additional comments:

Thanks! Please return your comments to: Marcia Jessen, Educational Ministries, ABC/USA, P.O. Box 851, Valley Forge, PA 19482-0851; 610-768-2056 FAX; marcia.jessen@abc-usa.org

Making an Action Plan

by Linda R. Isham

"I've got to say," Pastor Pat spoke up first, "I didn't think we could possibly do anything different with our teaching ministry. Now here we are, ready to divide up responsibilities on two new, exciting offerings. I'm really glad we worked on this."

Art Craft agreed, "I was just about to say the same thing. Frankly, I didn't think there really was anything different to do. It's sad to think about some of the things we're letting go, but I really like what we're planning."

"People talk to me, as you know, and they're saying the same thing," said Kate Ulater. "Some have even shared with me that they're willing to help out. Some of us are still not 100 percent sure about all this, and I still don't want us to change much, but I'm willing to try this out and see what happens."

Imogene Pozibel responded graciously, "Thanks for all your efforts. I know that this was really hard sometimes. I'm really pleased with where we are and excited about where we're going. And, more importantly, I think the Lord is pleased, too. Now, are we ready to look at the tasks that need to be done and who might do them?"

"I believe we are," said a newly hopeful Stuart Dent, and in his heart he believed that they really were. If I hadn't been here to experience all the work, I would think this was a miracle, *he thought.* But, then again, I guess there's something miraculous every time God is involved in our work.

———◆———

Making an action plan is all about making decisions and commitments to follow through on the teaching/learning actions, programs, and ministries you've been developing. It's where the rubber meets the road, so to speak. Now is the time to prioritize your menu of possibilities and get specific about next steps. The key word in this step is action. And this step moves you toward implementation. Just as there is a fine line between developing a menu of possible teaching/learning actions, programs, and ministries and making an action plan, there is a fine line between making an action plan and implementing the plan.

This step is intended to help you do several things: narrow down your list of possible teaching/learning actions, ministries, programs; identify one or two programs or actions for experimentation; and spell out what tasks are needed to implement actions, programs, or ministries in your prioritized menu of possibilities, who will do them, who else needs to know what you are going to be doing, and by when the task needs to be finished. If your actions, programs, and ministries are few and fairly simple and your church is small, your action plan can be fairly simple. If, however, your church is larger and your actions, programs, and ministries are many and more complex and lots of people and groups will be affected, your action plan will be more complex and this step will take more time.

Recording your decisions and plan in one place for all to see is important for a number of reasons: having a common understanding of decisions, making it public, building ownership, holding one another accountable, plus making it easier for duplicating and following up.

You'll want to begin by reviewing your possibilities and then prioritizing them, making sure they are in the order that makes sense for your situation. A process for doing this is outlined in the sidebar headed "Prioritizing Menu of Possibilities." A word of caution may be in order. Don't try to do everything at once. It's okay to be selective and to save some actions, ministries, and programs for a later time. In the course of your prioritizing work, you may see some programs or actions that lend themselves to experimentation. The sidebar headed "Experimentation" gives you some suggestions with regard to trying out something before committing to it long term. Once these tasks are accomplished, you can focus on identifying specific things that need to be done for each program, action, and ministry, who will do them, who else needs to know, and by when the tasks will be accomplished. The sidebar "Action Plan" has some suggestions for doing this.

Prioritizing Menu of Possibilities

Maaterials Needed: brainstorm list of possible teaching/learning actions, ministries, and programs; self-adhesive colored dots (available from an office supply store); newsprint, felt-tip markers, masking tape

Time Needed: 1½–2 hours

1. Pray for discernment.

2. Post your brainstorm list of possible teaching actions, ministries, programs.

3. Spend time seeking to understand the ideas shared, combining ideas where it seems appropriate, and doing whatever other analysis seems to make sense in terms of the list generated, the people present, and your situation. Now is the time for discussion of the merits of suggested actions, ministries, and programs. The questions on Reproducible Sheet 10 may be helpful at this point in the process. And you may think of others specific to your situation.

4. Give each person the opportunity to choose his or her priorities. One way to do this is to give every person in the group a number of self-adhesive colored dots (everyone gets the same number of the same color) to use in identifying the most important things for this congregation to do in/for its teaching ministry. The number of dots given is based on the number of items on the list to be prioritized. A rule of thumb is a dot for every ten items listed. So if your list has fifty items everyone gets five dots.

5. Once you've completed the ranking, stand back and count the dots. List the top items on a separate sheet of newsprint, starting with the items having the most dots. Often there will be clusters and the trends will be obvious. If this is not the case, you can have individuals do further ranking by choosing the three most important actions, ministries, and programs from those items just ranked.

6. Look at the ranked list and have further discussion. Sometimes further combination or groupings will be evident. And you may want to go back to the questions listed in number 3 above as you further your prioritizing work.

7. Consider whether any of the suggested teaching/learning actions, ministries, or programs would benefit by a period of experimentation to test their usefulness in your situation. Assign any experimentation to an individual or group to implement (see "Experimentation" box).

8. Affirm your prioritized list of teaching/learning actions, ministries, and programs and share prayers of thanksgiving.

Experimentation

1. Identify the actions, ministries, or programs that stand out as candidates for experimentation. Experimentation gives you a focused time to figure out some things and the opportunity to learn from either success or failure. Experimentation is particularly helpful if you are considering a major change with regard to an existing program or ministry—for instance, deciding to move the church school from Sunday to a weekday.

2. Select one or two items to try out for a short time. Don't take on too many!

3. Decide on the length of time of the experimentation, assign people to implement the experiment, get governing board approval, prepare the congregation, and develop a plan for evaluating. Involve participants in the evaluating.

As you think about people who might take on specific tasks, don't limit yourself to your planning group. It's a good idea to have as many of the potential implementers involved in planning as possible and therefore the broadest based planning group as possible. Keep in

mind others in your congregation who might have just the gifts needed to take on the tasks before you.

Just as you think about others who might have gifts needed for various programs, reflect on any constraints you face, such as limited financial resources or people and/or groups who might resist new actions and programs. Talk about how you can overcome such constraints. As you work on the action plan, be aware of the impact of your plan, or parts of it, on the rest of the life of your congregation. Note where connections need to be made with other groups, persons, or ministries. Give attention to any parts of your plan that may meet resistance. Anticipating the possibility of resistance now may

prevent a major problem later on. Plan ways to test out or experiment with these potential pinch points before making final commitments. As you identify potential points of resistance or constraint, you can list people that you'll want to talk with and/or involve. Building partnerships is one key to faithful and effective ministry implementation.

A worksheet (Reproducible Sheet 11) has been developed to guide you in making your action plan. Use the worksheet as is or modify it to suit your purposes. As a way of continuing with our Old New Century Church's planning, we have included a completed worksheet as a sample (see Figure 3).

Action Plan Worksheet

Figure 3

Action/Program/Ministry   *gifts identification program*

TASK	WHO WILL DO THIS	WHO NEEDS TO KNOW	DUE DATE
Find a leader for these sessions	Martha	Recruiting Team / Pastor	June 1
Choose materials, including a gifts inventory	Mary and Martha	Recruiting Team / Church Council	June 1
Set dates in September and following	Mary and Martha	Church office for calendar	June 15
Promote	Mary	Church Secretary	June 30
Ask pastor to preach on topic	Martha		July 1
Set up retrieval system	Mary	Recruiting Team / Church Secretary	September
Set up ongoing system for newcomers and current members who've not yet participated	Mary	Deacons / Church Council	September
Evaluation	Martha	Church Council / Recruiting Team	September

Action Plan

Materials Needed: prioritized list of teaching/learning actions, ministries, and programs; newsprint; felt-tip markers; masking tape; action plan worksheets

Time Needed: varies depending on the number of actions, ministries, and programs in your action plan

1. Gather your list of prioritized teaching actions, ministries, and programs. It is a good idea when working on this step in a group to work on newsprint before the whole group so that you have a common record and then later transfer the information from newsprint to separate sheets of paper.

2. Post a newsprint worksheet for each action, program, and ministry you will be working on.

3. Spend time in prayer as you begin and at appropriate points in the process.

4. For each action, program, or ministry, begin by listing the tasks that need to be done. Then go back, order them, and determine who will do each task, who else needs to know about this part of your action plan, and when each task needs to be done.

5. You could work in small groups, each working on an action, program, or ministry, thus accomplishing several at the same time. If you work this way, plan a time for the entire group to review the work of the small groups.

6. When your action plan is complete, pause for a time of thanksgiving and celebration.

Now with a plan in hand, it's time to put it into action—to take what started out as a dream or hope, was shaped into manageable actions, and give it feet and wings. Know that as you implement your plans you are not alone. You have many partners both near and far and God's presence to continue to guide and uphold you. Remember the words of 2 Corinthians 4:1, "Therefore, since it is by God's mercy that we are engaged in this ministry, we do not lose heart" (NRSV).

We wish you grace and wisdom.

Praying...
for Making an Action Plan

Pray that in the midst of the business at hand you will

> listen to one another,
> hear God's word anew,
> sense Christ's presence,
> let "our souls catch up with our bodies."

Invite the congregation to be in prayer with you, to be prayer partners.

Use any of the following prayer resources or those from your own rich storehouse.

- Make Roberta Porter's poem your prayer.

  Emmaus Change

  After all—
  the death, loss
  mourning, and mystery,
  after Easter's miracle
  and word of new life,
  they met a man
  on the road to Emmaus.

  In the teaching, leading,
  walking,
  they marveled at his wisdom
  and finally,
  in the breaking of bread,
  their eyes were opened—
  they recognized Christ
  and were changed.

  And today
  in all the meetings,
  committees, decisions,
  in the teaching, cooking,
  planning,
  could we also stop,
  give thanks
  and be changed,
  to see each other,
  and to recognize among us
  the presence
  and the leading
  of our Lord.

Roberta Porter (*Alive Now,* March/April 1998, 52–53.) Used by permission.

- Pray

  that God's Spirit working in our hearts will transform the actions, programs, and ministries into more than a list of things to do,
  that we will see ways to use these actions, programs, and ministries for the common good,
  that in implementing these actions, programs, and ministries we will be servant leaders.

- Give thanks

  for hard work
  for perseverance
  for many gifts freely shared
  for working together
  for deep, rich thinking and dialogue
  for the faith community's support
  for the presence of the One who has gone before, goes with us now, and will be with us in the future.
  Amen.

Learning...
for Making an Action Plan

- Begin a study on leadership. Making, interpreting, and implementing an action plan requires strong and faithful leadership. Explore what it means to be spiritual leaders. See this chapter's **RESOURCES** for suggested resources to use in your study.

- Contact other churches to find out
  - how they go about making an action plan for their teaching ministry
  - what they have learned about preparing to interpret and implement new programs or actions
  - how they meet and overcome resistance and challenges to changes in programming
  - what are some key ingredients in successfully and faithfully implementing an action plan

- Learn ways to meet resistance and overcome constraints you face. See this chapter's **RESOURCES**.

Sharing...
for Making an Action Plan

Plan on sharing one-on-one, with the gathered community, with key groups and leaders.

Use any or all of the following ways to communicate with and/or involve the congregation.

1. Post minutes from your meetings.
2. Put brief articles in your church newsletter, on the church web site (if your church has one), and in the worship bulletin.
3. Talk with other members informally and one-on-one about what you are working on.
4. Give attention to the points of resistance and learn from those encounters.
5. Invite others to join you in working on the details of your action plan.
6. Be thinking about and inviting people to join you in implementing the action plan.
7. If you have chosen to experiment with an action or program, keep in mind the importance of the following:

   - setting a specific length of time for the experiment
   - preparing people for the experiment with information in many ways and places, anticipating questions and providing answers
   - giving ample notice of the planned experiment
   - continuing to share information and reports during the period of experimentation
   - evaluating the experiment—involving as many people as possible in this—and sharing the results, next steps, and decisions made

Resources...
for Making an Action Plan

On Leadership

Alive Now, March/April 1998. This issue focuses on spiritual leadership. Single copy $3. To order, call 1-800-925-6847.

De Pree, Max, *Leadership Is an Art,* (New York: Doubleday, 1989). Looks at leadership as liberating people to do what is required of them in the most effective and human way possible, encouraging contrary opinions and abandoning oneself to the strength of others.

De Pree, Max, *Leading Without Power: Finding Hope in Serving Community,* (San Francisco: Jossey-Bass, 1997). Offers hope and encouragement for creating communities that inspire the best in people.

Greenleaf, Robert K., Anne T. Fraker, and Larry C. Spears, editors, *Seeker and Servant: Reflections on Religious Leadership,* (San Francisco: Jossey-Bass, 1996). This collection of essays expands on Greenleaf's servant-leadership theme, examines his belief that churches should be the most useful change agents in our society, and details the importance of personal spirituality.

Morris, Danny E., and Charles M. Olsen, *Discerning God's Will Together: A Spiritual Practice for the Church,* (Nashville: The Upper Room, 1997). Presents discernment as an interactive decision-making process and uses examples of a small group, a congregation, and a judicatory.

Olsen, Charles M., *Transforming Church Boards into Communities of Spiritual Leaders,* (Bethesda, MD: The Alban Institute, 1995). $15.75. Provides a model for working on church boards or committees that can be fulfilling instead of draining—shared stories, Scripture, prayer, and discernment.

Pathways Network, a new Christian initiative connecting lay and clergy church leaders, launched by The Upper Room—a network, events, and resources. Annual membership $50. For more information, visit the Pathways home page at: **www.upperroom.org/pathways** or write to Pathways Network, The Upper Room, P.O. Box 189, Nashville, TN 37202.

Rinehart, Stacy T., *Upside Down: The Paradox of Servant Leadership,* (Colorado Springs: NavPress, 1998). A look at power versus servanthood in leadership.

On Overcoming Resistance and Constraints

Friend, Howard E. Jr., *Recovering the Sacred Center: Church Renewal from the Inside Out,* (Valley Forge, PA: Judson Press, 1998). See especially chapter 11 and the conclusion, which describes a case study.

Comment Sheet

We are eager to learn from users what has been helpful, has worked or not, or could have worked better, as well as what you have been able to accomplish with the help of this resource. Please take a few minutes to respond to the following questions and then send them to the address listed below. Use additional pages as needed.

1. These comments are in response to the following steps/chapters [please check the appropriate step(s) or chapter(s)]:

    ___Seeing the Big Picture and Getting Started
    ___Picturing the Future
    ___Stating Our Mission
    ___Assessing Our Situation
    ___Shaping a Vision
    ___Celebrating and Letting Go
    ___Developing a Menu of Possibilities
    ___Making an Action Plan

2. The most helpful part of this step in the planning process was . . .

3. The least helpful part of this step in the planning process was . . .

4. Changes you should consider are . . .

5. Consider adding the following resource(s) to the resource list:

6. Our key accomplishments related to this step of the planning process are . . .

7. Additional comments:

Thanks! Please return your comments to: Marcia Jessen, Educational Ministries, ABC/USA, P.O. Box 851, Valley Forge, PA 19482-0851; 610-768-2056 FAX; marcia.jessen@abc-usa.org

Denominational Contact Information

American Baptist Churches, USA

To order or inquire about curriculum resources, books, or other Christian education resources, contact:

Judson Press
P. O. Box 851
Valley Forge, PA 19482-0851
1-800-4-JUDSON
610-768-2107 FAX
www.judsonpress.com
Judson offers a complete line of Sunday school curriculum and other resources for American Baptist congregations, as well as *Baptist Leader, The Secret Place, The African American Pulpit,* and a variety of books for the entire Christian community.

To inquire about workshops, training events, or resources related to Christian education or leader development, contact:

Educational Ministries
American Baptist Churches, USA
P. O. Box 851
Valley Forge, PA 19482-0851
1-800-ABC-3USA, menu selection #8
610-768-2056 FAX
www.abc-em.org
Educational Ministries offers assistance in the following specialized areas: children, youth, young adult, and adult ministries; African American and Hispanic Christian education; leader development; and congregational education.

To inquire about demographic information on your community, contact:

Director of Planning Resources
National Ministries, ABC/USA
P. O. Box 851
Valley Forge, PA 19482-0851
1-800-ABC-3USA, ext. 2494
610-768-2453 FAX

Presbyterian Church (U.S.A.)

To order or inquire about curriculum resources, books, or other Christian education resources, contact:

Curriculum Publishing Program Area (CPPA)
100 Witherspoon Street
Louisville, KY 40202-1396
800-929-2632
502-569-8329 FAX
http://www.pcusa.org/pcusa/currpub
CPPA offers a full line of curriculum products, including the denomination's official curriculum, Covenant People, and provides electronic, print, and audiovisual publications under its two imprints, Bridge Resources (ecumenical products) and Witherspoon Press (Reformed and Presbyterian-specific products).

Cumberland Presbyterian Church

To order or inquire about curriculum resources, books, or other Christian education resources, contact:

Cumberland Presbyterian Resource Center
1978 Union Avenue
Memphis, TN 38104-4134
1-800-333-2772
901-276-6288 FAX
book@cumberland.org
This is the Cumberland Presbyterian source for ordering curriculum resources and other materials.

To inquire about workshops, training events, or resources related to Christian education or leader development, contact:

Board of Christian Education
1978 Union Avenue
Memphis, TN 38104-4134
901-276-4572
901-272-3913 FAX
The Board of Christian Education offers assistance in leader development and support, curriculum selection, and specialized ministries with children, youth, and adults.

To inquire about demographic information on your community, contact:

Church Growth and Evangelism Unit
Board of Missions
1978 Union Avenue
Memphis, TN 38104-4134
901-276-4572, ext. 3334
901-276-4578 FAX

The United Church of Canada

To order or inquire about curriculum resources, books, or other Christian education resources, contact:

United Church Publishing House
Distribution Centre
25 Connell Court, Unit #2
Toronto, Ontario M8Z 1E8
1-800-288-7635
416-253-5456
416-253-1630 FAX

To inquire about books and resources published by the United Church Publishing House and the United Church of Canada, please contact:

United Church Publishing House
The United Church of Canada
3250 Bloor Street West
Toronto, Ontario M8X 2Y4
416-231-5931, ext. 4086
416-232-6004 FAX
bookpub@uccan.org
www.uccan.org
The United Church Publishing House offers a unique selection of books and resources for individual and congregational use in the areas of worship, Christian education for all ages, spiritual nurture, women in ministry and social action. We mail throughout North America. Catalogues available upon request.

A Guide for Reshaping Your Church's Teaching Ministry

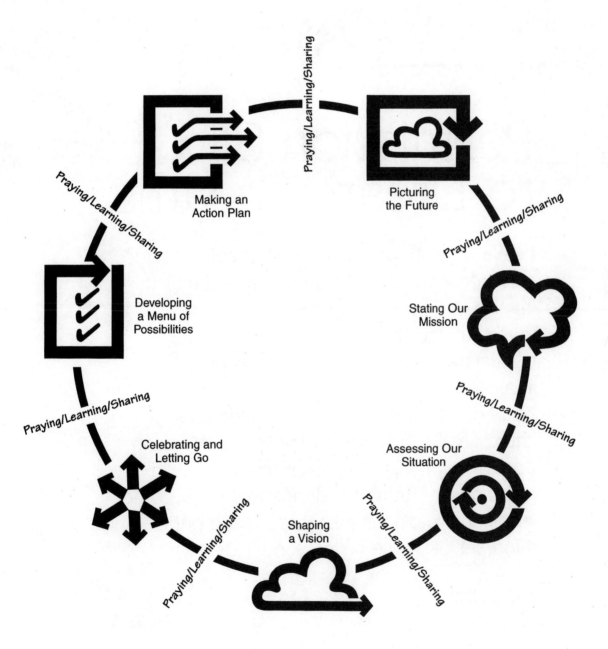

Picturing the Future

Stating Our Mission

Assessing Our Situation

Shaping a Vision

Celebrating and Letting Go

Developing a Menu of Possibilities

Making an Action Plan

Praying/Learning/Sharing

Permission Slip to Dream Dreams...

I give myself permission to dream dreams and create new visions. I understand that this may involve letting go of past images and opening myself to the direction of the Holy Spirit. I understand that I am allowed to pray, think, imagine, create, dream–vision, and search for all kinds of possibilities for the teaching ministry of the church. Nothing is impossible for all things are possible with God. The only restriction while picturing the future (or during any of the other steps of this planning process) is the phrase and the mind-set of "we've never done it that way before."

Signature

Date

Engaging the Biblical Texts

Mark 12:28-31; Matthew 18:18-20; Mark 4:21-25; Luke 1:26-38

Reflection Questions

Who are the characters?

What is the flow of events? (look before/after the text for more of the story)

What are some key words or phrases in the text?

What is the God-given mission spelled out in the text?

What is the response of the person or people called?

What is the outcome?

Understanding the Shifting World

1. From independent economies limited by national and political boundaries to one global economy transcending political and national borders:

- Think of an example of what impact this has on you locally.

- How might your teaching mission address this?

2. From a focus on sports as the primary leisure activity to a focus on the visual and performance arts:

- Think of an example of what impact this has on you locally.

- How might your teaching mission address this?

3. From the classical, Marxist socialism of the collective to "capitalist socialism" allowing individual entrepreneurship:

- Think of an example of what impact this has on you locally.

- How might your teaching mission address this?

4. From national and ethnic differences in lifestyles to a homogenizing of world cultures (with an accompanying nationalist backlash):

- Think of an example of what impact this has on you locally.

- How might your teaching mission address this?

5. From government-run welfare systems to privatized "workfare" systems:

- Think of an example of what impact this has on you locally.

- How might your teaching mission address this?

6. From trade centered in Europe and North America to trade centered in the Pacific Rim nations:

- Think of an example of what impact this has on you locally.

- How might your teaching mission address this?

7. From traditional, male-dominated business practices to innovative, female-led business practices:

- Think of an example of what impact this has on you locally.

- How might your teaching mission address this?

8. From understanding the world as a series of mechanical operations to understanding the world as the interaction of organic systems:

- Think of an example what impact this has on you locally.

- How might your teaching mission address this?

9. From the dominance of science over religion to the reemergence of significant religious belief (with the continuing decline of traditional mainline religious practice):

- Think of an example of what impact this has on you locally.

- How might your teaching mission address this?

10. From the era of "The Movement," when groups influence change to a new understanding of the importance of the individual in societal change:

- Think of an example of what impact this has on you locally.

- How might your teaching mission address this?

11. From an organized religion-based culture (U.S.), where traditional religious affiliation is acceptable, or at least benignly tolerated, to a secular culture that is at best suspicious of organized religion and at worst openly hostile toward it:

- Think of an example of what impact this has on you locally.

- How might your teaching mission address this?

Developing Your Provisional Teaching Mission Statement

Given all that we as a group have discovered, discussed, and prayed about, consider the following questions:

1. With whom might our teaching mission be involved? What group of people are we called to reach?

2. What might be the focus of our teaching mission with these people?

3. What am I most passionate about in my Christian faith? What do I feel other people should not miss in their spiritual journey?

4. As a preliminary starting point, I would sum up our mission this way—"Our teaching mission is . . ."

1. Statistical information.

Average worship attendance   _____

Average Sunday school attendance   _____

Number of resident members   _____

Average age of active participants   _____

Average age of Sunday school participants   _____

2. Beliefs. What are the basic Christian beliefs of our congregation?

One means of studying the theology of a church is to look at the church's constitution, statement of faith, or mission statement. Another possibility involves using the following questions as a basis for group discussion. Other questions could be added.

1. "Faith" has meant many different things to people. Which one of the following statements do you believe **comes closest** to describing our church's view of faith? (Circle one response only.)

    a. A life of commitment to God that I demonstrate by trying to do what is right.

    b. My decision to accept Christ instead of going on in my own sinful ways.

    c. My trust in God's grace.

    d. My belief in all that the Bible says.

    e. In my view, as long as people are truly sincere in their beliefs, they show faith.

    f. I am not sure what "faith" means, although I am convinced that it is important.

    g. To be honest about it, the idea of faith doesn't seem very meaningful to me.

    h. None of these. What faith means to us is . . .

2. Which one of the following do you believe **comes closest** to our church's view of the way in which God influences the things that happen in the world? (Circle only one response.)

    a. God sets history in motion but really doesn't interfere with it anymore.

    b. God influences individuals, who then shape events.

    c. God influences individuals but also shapes events directly through nations and social affairs.

    d. I don't think of God as "influencing" the things that happen.

    e. Not sure because I haven't thought about it much before.

    f. None of these. Our view is . . .

3. People often wonder how a merciful God can allow terrible things to happen, such as the killing of six million Jews during World War II. Which statement do you believe **comes closest** to our church's view of why God lets these things happen? (Circle only one response.)

    a. God allows terrible things to happen to punish people for their sins.

    b. We don't know why these things happen, but we know that God is able to use them for good.

    c. God doesn't have anything to do with these things; the devil causes them.

    d. People cause these things to happen, not God.

    e. Frankly, I don't know how God can allow these things to happen; it doesn't seem right to me.

    f. I don't have a view on this topic.

    g. None of the above. Our view is . . .

4. Which one of the following statements do you believe **comes closest** to expressing our church's view of life after death? (Circle only one.)

    a. I don't believe there is life after death.

    b. I am unsure whether there is life after death.

    c. I believe that there must be something beyond death, but I have no idea what it may be like.

    d. There is life after death but no punishment.

    e. There is life after death with rewards for some people and punishment for others.

    f. The notion of reincarnation expresses our view of what happens to people when they die.

    g. None of these. What we think about life after death is . . .

5. Which of these statements do you believe **comes closest** to describing our church's feelings about the Bible? (Circle only one.)

    a. The Bible is the actual word of God and is to be taken literally, word for word.

    b. The Bible is the inspired word of God, but not everything in it should be taken literally, word for word.

    c. The Bible is an ancient book of fables, legends, history, and moral precepts recorded by men.

    d. Can't say.

    e. None of these. Our view is . . .

6. Which one of the following do you believe **comes closest** to our church's attitude toward people in other countries who have never heard about Christ?

    a. A desire to share the love of Christ with them.

    b. A feeling that if we do not preach Christ to them, they will be damned forever.

    c. A feeling that we shouldn't worry about them because there are so many people in this country who haven't heard about Christ.

    d. A feeling that we should respect their religions and stop trying to impose Christianity on them.

    e. Frankly, I haven't thought about it.

    f. Can't choose.

7. Christians sometimes describe God as a "God of justice" or a God who commands us to bring about justice. Which one of the following statements do you believe **comes closest** to our church's ideas about what this means? (Circle only one.)

    a. It means that the church should work for justice and support groups that are working to end inequality and oppression.

    b. It means we should try to be just and fair in all our dealings.

    c. This is actually a spiritual term that refers to God punishing evil, rather than activities of the church or individuals.

    d. Frankly, the concept of God's justice doesn't have any particular meaning to me.

    e. I'm not really sure what it refers to.

    f. None of these. Its meaning to us is . . .

3. **Rituals.** Repetitive actions through which a group communicates its meaning and identity.

What are the rituals that take place in the life of our congregation? (From welcoming persons as they enter the building, to birthday cakes for children, to baptismal confessions, to lighting the Advent wreath.)

Which rituals take place weekly?

Which rituals are seasonal?

4. **Symbols.** Objects that stand for something else.

There are symbols in each church that nearly everyone understands as he or she comes through the door, for example, the cross, the altar, the communion elements. Each church also has symbols that are unique to its own congregation.

List as many symbols you can think of that are central to our church's identity. Put a 1 beside the symbols that everyone knows and understands. Put a 2 beside the symbols that only persons with faith and/or with a church affiliation would understand. Put a 3 beside the symbols that only persons in your church would understand.

5. **What is the character of our church?** What is the "personality" of our church? What makes us unique? How are we alike and different from other churches in our denomination and our community?

Planning for Effective and Vital Christian Education[5]
An Assessment Tool

1. Rate your congregation's Christian education by putting the appropriate numeral on the blank to the left of each statement:

    1 = strong
    2 = adequate
    3 = needs improvement
    4 = not applicable

    Note that there is space to add additional descriptive statements.

2. Review your ratings and from among all twelve characteristics, star (*) the three needing attention first.

3. In the right-hand column, "Concerns/Next Steps," jot down concerns you have or steps you think could be taken.

Characteristics of Effective and Vital Christian Education	Concerns/Next Steps
___ 1. **This church gives priority to Christian education (CE) and understands that it is more than just Sunday church school.** ___ adequate financial support given ___ frequent mention of CE in public places ___ adequate time set aside for formal CE ___ informal teaching and learning recognized and affirmed ___ Christian education takes place in a variety of settings (committees, choirs, worship, special events, etc.) ___ sees CE as belonging to the church, not just to teachers or the CE board ___	
___ 2. **The staff is committed to, involved in, and equipped for Christian education.** ___ teach ___ attend CE board meeting ___ advocate for CE ___ preach teaching sermons ___ support teachers and leaders ___ give strong leadership ___ work in partnership with volunteers ___	
___ 3. **Teachers and leaders are knowledgeable, committed, caring, passionate, and open to learning.** ___ attend training events ___ tend to their own spiritual growth ___ spend time outside class with those they teach ___ are themselves open to learning and growing ___ are prepared ___ know the Bible and teaching methods ___ keep abreast of current information and skills ___ see themselves as partners in an important ministry ___	

___ 4. **The teaching ministry with adults is given strong emphasis.**
___ choices of study offered
___ in-depth Bible study available
___ small groups provided
___ in auxiliary groups, boards, committees, choirs
___ church membership/discipleship classes
___ addresses faith issues and needs of adults
___ challenges adults to grow in faith maturity
___

___ 5. **Programs for children are offered.**
___ during Sunday church school
___ during the week, after school or evening
___ weekday nursery school and/or child care
___ camping opportunities for elementary age children
___ choirs or musical groups
___ church membership/discipleship classes for older
  elementary children
___ addresses faith development needs of children
  in ways appropriate to age
___ challenges children to grow in faith
___

___ 6. **Programs for youth are offered.**
___ classes during Sunday church school
___ evening fellowship group(s)
___ camp and conference opportunities
___ college, career, and/or job counseling
___ mentoring
___ church membership/discipleship classes
___ addresses faith development needs of youth
___ challenges youth to grow in faith
___

___ 7. **The content offered for study addresses:**
___ biblical knowledge, understanding, and application
___ global awareness
___ moral and value issues
___ social and justice issues
___ spiritual development
___ issues relevant to students
___ people being able to share with others what their faith means
___ faith development in age or faith maturity
  appropriate ways
___

___ 8. **A variety of learning opportunities is used for all ages.**
___ AV and electronic equipment available
___ resource center available
___ teachers use stories, drama, visuals, activities, etc.
___ teachers encouraged to use a variety of
  methods and to try new methods
___ mission tours, work groups, and service projects
  included as learning activities
___

____ 9. **Strong administrative foundations are in place.**
   ____ teacher/leader recruitment based on gifts
   ____ teacher/leader recognition
   ____ teacher/leader training
   ____ teacher/leader support
   ____ teacher/leader faith formation (spiritual growth)
   ____ mission and vision statements guide planning and are known
   ____ program goals and objectives are stated and known
   ____ evaluation done regularly
   ____ time for silence, prayer, and discernment is allotted
   ____ structures empower rather than drain people

   ____

____ 10. **Parents and guardians are supported in their "teaching" roles.**
   ____ family worship ideas (including special seasons such
         as Advent, Lent) provided
   ____ parenting classes offered
   ____ Bible study groups for parents offered
   ____ family life center provided

   ____

____ 11. **Members are informed, eager, and enthusiastic
   about the teaching ministry.**
   ____ are involved as participants
   ____ invite new people to attend
   ____ offer to help carry out the teaching ministry
   ____ undergird the ministry with prayer
   ____ regularly show appreciation to those giving
         leadership in the teaching ministry

   ____

____ 12. **Education reaches out and addresses the needs of
   the immediate community.**

   ____
   ____
   ____
   ____
   ____

The twelve focus statements listed above will not only help you evaluate where your church's teaching ministry is right now, but will help clarify some new directions for the future.

[5] adapted from Isham, Linda, *"Planning for Effective and Vital Christian Education,"* appendix A, *The Teaching Church at Work: A Manual for the Board of Christian Education* (Valley Forge: Judson Press, 1993). Used by permission.

A Vision for the Future

"Write the vision; make it plain on tablets, so that a runner may read it.
For there is still a vision for the appointed time."

(Habakkuk 2:2b-3a, NRSV)

A vision statement . . .

grows out of a mission statement,
gives future legs to a mission statement,
is future-oriented,
speaks about how we'll look and/or what we'll do,
is hopeful,
comes from spending time discerning what God would have us do,
becomes a bridge from the past into the future.

Criteria:

1. Describe the vision in terms of the future.

2. State it clearly and in a compelling way (so that someone who did not write it can understand and commit himself or herself to it).

3. Use vivid language and make it motivational.

4. Keep it short!

Examples:

A man on the moon by the end of the decade. (John F. Kennedy)

A personal computer in every home that everyone can use. (Bill Gates)

Give attention to those not now part of our faith community.
Reclaim our courage and heart for teaching the faith.
Orchestrate ways for people to learn to be a transforming presence in the world.
Walk with those we call to lead and teach others.

("Old New Century Church")

Brainstorming Guidelines

1. **Set a time limit.**

2. **Everyone gets to speak.**

3. **No editing.**

4. **No discussion or debate.**

5. **Ideas may be built upon.**

Mutual Invitation

If you have some people who tend to dominate in a group and others who are hesitant to speak, follow a procedure of mutual invitation whereby you start and share an idea and then invite the next person, who in turn invites someone else who has not spoken to speak, until all who want to have spoken. A person may choose to pass but even then has the opportunity to invite someone else to speak.

Prioritizing Questions

How will this action, ministry, or program help accomplish your mission and vision?

What is most important?

What needs to be done first?

What can be done quickly, easily, and be immediately useful, giving us some up-front energy?

What would take more time, development, and/or money?

How is the biblical message communicated in this action, ministry, or program?

How does this action, ministry, or program help individuals and this faith community remember who they are as people of God, who they are called to be, and what they are called to do in the future?

How does this action, ministry, or program help the congregation build community? help individuals and the congregation make faith meaningful in their lives? help nurture Christian hope?

Action Plan Worksheet

Action/Program/Ministry_____

_____

Task	Who Will Do This	Who Needs To Know	Due Date